Managing Trauma Workbook

A TOOLBOX of REPRODUCIBLE ASSESSMENTS and ACTIVITIES for Facilitators

Ester R.A. Leutenberg
and John J. Liptak, EdD

Duluth, Minnesota

101 W. 2nd St., Suite 203
Duluth, MN 55802

800-247-6789

books@wholeperson.com
www.wholeperson.com

Managing Trauma Workbook
A Toolbox of Reproducible Assessments and Activities
for Facilitators.

Copyright ©2015 by Ester R.A. Leutenberg and John J. Liptak.
All rights reserved. Except for short excerpts for review purposes and materials in the activities and handouts sections, no part of this workbook may be reproduced or transmitted in any form by any means, electronic or mechanical without permission in writing from the publisher. Activities and handouts are meant to be photocopied.

All efforts have been made to ensure accuracy of the information contained in this book as of the date published.
The author(s) and the publisher expressly disclaim responsibility for any adverse effects arising from the use or application of the information contained herein.

Printed in the United States of America

10 9 8 7 6 5 4 3 2 1

Editorial Director: Carlene Sippola
Art Director: Joy Morgan Dey
Assistant Art Director: Mathew Pawlak

Library of Congress Control Number: 2015940886
ISBN: 978-157025-334-8

Introduction

Using the *Managing Trauma Workbook*

Not everyone who experiences a traumatic event will necessarily suffer stress after trauma. People who experience a trauma may have very different reactions. Some may not experience any effects at all, while some will experience some effects because they are resilient, have a great support system, and have access to resources to help them. These people may not experience many, if any, symptoms of stress after a trauma.

For others, however, the effect of the trauma is significant and they experience stress as a result of their trauma. Often people who go through a personal event involving actual trauma, or who are exposed to an overwhelmingly stressful event or series of events, will continue to emotionally and physically re-experience the event and suffer from it over and over again, possibly for a long time.

Trauma can be life-changing. The activities in the *Managing Trauma Workbook* can be a tremendous benefit to anyone who has experienced a trauma.

There are many events that people perceive as stressful and that can cause stress as a result of having experienced them, however they are too numerous and too individualized to describe.

Some of the most common events include:

- Almost drowning
- Attack by animals
- Bombing
- Car or plane crash
- Child abuse or neglect
- Chronic disease or illness
- Criminal assault
- Cult abuse
- Earthquake
- Emotional abuse
- Explosion
- Fire
- Flood
- Incest
- Kidnapping
- Loss, or loss of use, of a body part
- Mugging
- Natural Disaster
- Nuclear disaster
- Physical abuse
- Physical proximity to a tragedy
- Rape
- Riots
- Sexual abuse
- Sudden life-threatening illness
- Terrorist attack
- Threat to safety
- Threatened with weapon
- Torture
- Verbal abuse
- War
- Witnessing a crime
- Witnessing a murder
- Witnessing anything terrible
- Witnessing suicide or attempted suicide

Factors that Affect Responses to Trauma

There are a wide variety of factors that affect the ways people respond to traumatic events.

Some of these factors include:

- **Prior knowledge** – People who know about a traumatic event before it happens tend to have less severe reactions. For example, if people knew that a hurricane was going to hit their city, they would have more time to prepare themselves physically, emotionally and psychologically.

- **Individual reactions** – Biological, emotional and environmental factors affect responses to trauma.

- **Number of events** – The more traumatic events people have, the greater their propensity for experiencing reactions.

- **Damage done** – The greater the damage to people, the more they are likely to have reactions.

- **The source** – The degree of inhumanity in the perpetration of the traumatic event.

- **Degree of responsibility** – People who feel responsible for causing or failing to prevent an event are more likely to have reactions.

How Does Trauma Manifest Itself?

Everyone experiences stress, but not all people experience the severe disruptive stress reactions associated with experiencing traumatic events. The difference between the experience of traumatic events and regular, ordinary stressful events depends on the perception of the events and individualized reactions. The level of inhumanity is significant. People may feel more traumatized by a violent crime than by nature's earthquake. Some are traumatized by a near-miss vehicle accident; others by serving in combat. Each person's experience is valid and treatable.

Because there are so many ways stress from traumatic events can manifest itself, these types of symptoms can be very difficult to identify and manage. It is critical to be aware of, and to understand, how these symptoms are commonly experienced.

Although most or all symptoms do not have to be present, those that are present will typically cause significant distress and/or impairment in a person's daily functioning.

Possible symptoms are listed on the next page.

Introduction

How Does Trauma Manifest Itself? *(Continued)*

Some of the many symptoms that interfere with daily functioning:

- Experiencing upsetting memories of the event that interfere with daily functioning
- Having flashbacks and feelings that the event is happening again
- Experiencing nightmares related to the event
- Feeling intense pain and/or distress when reminded of the event
- Having intense physical reactions when reminded of the event
- Avoiding people and places that are reminders of the event
- Feeling detached from others
- Feeling emotionally numb, or avoiding thoughts and feelings that are reminders
- Inability to remember important aspects of the trauma
- Losing interest in life
- Losing interest in activities that at one time were pleasurable
- Sensing that a future that was once imagined is no longer attainable
- Failing to fall or stay asleep
- Having outbursts of anger
- Feeling irritable
- Experiencing concentration, focus and memory problems
- Fear of additional threats
- Feeling jumpy and easily startled
- Engaging in impulsive and risky behavior
- *Zoning out* for short periods of time

Losing interest in life and in activities that were once pleasurable, plus some of the above and additional symptoms, may relate to traumatic events and/or other mental health issues.

Our goal for this workbook is NOT to diagnose a mental illness, nor do we expect the facilitator to make that diagnosis from this workbook's content. Our goal is to touch on some of the symptoms and possibilities of trauma, create realizations, and provide coping methods which will help people to go forward and perhaps to consider the possible need for medications and/or therapy.

Our goal is also to help participants recognize that other people have the similar issues, that no shame is connected to them, and that mental health issues of any degree are not to be stigmatized nor should anyone feel like victims to stereotyping.

In *Managing Trauma Workbook*, we use the phrase *mental health issues* **to include all types and levels of trauma issues.**

Helping People Cope with Reactions to a Trauma

Trauma survivors display complex sets of symptoms that need to be addressed if they are to heal. Following are some of the ways that facilitators can assist their clients in processing traumatic events, learning to manage the symptoms of trauma, and beginning the transition to a more satisfied life.

- Help participants learn as much as possible about reactions to trauma.

- Help participants explore their traumatic event in a structured, safe way – if a mental health professional believes the process will be therapeutic for an individual.

- Help participants accept their traumatic event and the impact these events have on their lives while focusing on the importance of taking actions to cope with the reactions to traumatic stress.

- Help participants see the importance of being proactive in coping with the stress associated with their traumatic events.

- Help participants understand that recovery from traumatic events will not happen immediately, but will happen a little at a time.

- Help participants accept that the purpose may not necessarily be to forget their traumatic events, but rather to accept what happened and learn to cope with the issues they are experiencing.

- Help participants understand and develop a plan for recognizing and coping with both the physical, emotional, psychological and interpersonal symptoms that they are experiencing.

- Help participants learn to identify the triggers that bring on reactions to their traumatic stress, and learn to cope with these triggers.

- Help participants learn skills for making the transition to a more manageable and satisfying life.

Introduction

How the *Managing Trauma Workbook* Can Help

People who have experienced a traumatic event are likely to develop a variety of symptoms associated with that event. The assessments and activities in this workbook are designed to provide facilitators with a wide variety of tools to use in helping people manage their lives more effectively. Many choices for self-exploration are provided for facilitators to determine which tools best suit the unique needs of their clients.

The purpose of this workbook is to provide a user-friendly guide to short-term assessments and activities to help people manage their issues related to trauma, and experience a greater sense of well-being. In addition, this workbook is designed to help provide facilitators and participants with tools and information needed to overcome the stigma attached to the reactions of trauma issues.

In order to help participants successfully deal with reactions to traumatic events, facilitators need to have a variety of assessments and activities to help their participants open-up and begin to manage the symptoms of traumatic issues. The Managing Trauma Workbook provides assessments and self-guided activities to help participants understand the intensity of their issues and how can lead a more effective life.

When to Worry?

The symptoms related to traumatic events can be very complex and difficult to cope with. The good news is that people can develop symptom management skills and progress toward more satisfying lives. The symptoms that accompany traumatic event issues that people deal with daily can be a very frightening way to live. **People who experience this over time are at risk of having a serious mental illness and need to seek a medical professional.**

Suicide Warning!

Many trauma survivors feel suicidal, have suicidal thoughts, and make plans for committing suicide. Sometimes they think that the only way to escape the physical, psychological, and emotional pain is to attempt suicide. Remember to take any talk about suicide or suicidal acts very seriously.

Signs of suicidal thoughts:
- Withdrawing from family, friends, and activities of interest in the past
- Increasing use of harmful substances
- Giving away possessions
- Expressing severe hopelessness about the future
- Making a plan to die by suicide
- Calling or visiting people to say goodbye
- Getting legal affairs in order
- Engaging in reckless actions
- Talking about killing or harming self
- Expressing feelings of being trapped with no way out
- Purchasing a weapon

Serious Mental Illness

If participants have a serious mental illness, they need to do much more than complete the assessments, activities and exercises contained in this workbook. They need to be taken seriously and facilitators can take an active role in their finding help immediately. All disturbances of thoughts, feelings and actions need to be thoroughly evaluated by a medical professional, and then treated with an appropriate combination of medication and group and/or individual therapy.

Format of the *Managing Trauma Workbook*

The *Managing Trauma Workbook* is designed to be used either independently or as part of an established mental health issue program. You may administer any of the assessments and the guided self-exploration activities to an individual or a group with whom you are working, and you may administer any of the assessments and activities over one or more days. Feel free to pick and choose those that best fit the outcomes you desire. The purpose of this workbook is to provide facilitators who work with individuals and groups who may be experiencing issues related to traumatic events with a series of reproducible activities that can used to supplement their work with participants. Because these activity pages are reproducible, they can be photocopied as is, or you may adapt them by whiting out and writing in your own changes to suit the need of each group, using that page as your master to be photocopied for each participant

Assessments
Assessments establish a behavioral baseline from which facilitators and participants can gauge progress toward identified goals. This workbook will supplement facilitator's work by providing assessments designed to measure behavioral baselines for evaluating client change. In order to do so, assessments with scoring directions and interpretation materials begin each chapter. The authors recommend that you begin presenting each topic by asking participants to complete the assessment. Facilitators can choose one or more, or all of the activities relevant to their participants' specific needs and concerns.

Each of the awareness modules contained in this book begin with an assessment for these purposes:
- Help facilitators to develop a numerical baseline of behavior, attitude and personality characteristics before they begin their plan of treatment.
- Help facilitators gather valuable information about their participants.
- Help facilitators in the measurement of change over time.
- Use as pre-tests and post-tests to measure changes in behavior, attitude, and personality.
- Help facilitators identify patterns that are negatively affecting a participant.
- Prompt insight and behavioral change.
- Assist participants to feel a part of the treatment-planning process.
- Provide participants with a starting point to begin to learn more about themselves and their strengths and limitations.

Assessments are a great aid in developing plans for effective change.
Be aware of the following when administering, scoring, and interpreting the assessments in this book:
- The purpose of these assessments is not to pigeonhole people, but to allow them to explore various elements of themselves and their situations.
- This book contains self-assessments and not tests. Traditional tests measure knowledge or right or wrong responses. For the assessments provided in this workbook, remind participants that there are no right or wrong answers. These assessments ask only for opinions or attitudes.
- The assessments in this workbook have face value, but have not been formally normed for validity and reliability.
- The assessments in this workbook are based on self-reported data. In other words, the accuracy and usefulness of the information is dependent on the information that participants honestly provide about themselves. Assure them that they do not need to share their information with anyone. They can be honest!
- Remind participants that the assessments are exploratory exercises and not a judgment of who they are as human beings.
- The assessments are not a substitute for professional assistance. If you feel any of your participants need more assistance than you can provide, refer them to an appropriate medical professional.

Format of the Managing Trauma Workbook (Continued)
Assessment Script

When administering the assessments contained in this workbook, please remember that the assessments can be administered, scored, and interpreted by the client. If working in a group, facilitators should circulate among participants as they complete assessments to ensure that there are no questions. If working with an individual client, facilitators can use the instruction collaboratively.

Please note that as your participants begin the assessments in this workbook, the participants' instructions italicized below are meant to be a guide, so please do not feel you must read or say them word for word.

Tell your participants: *"You will be completing a quick assessment related to the topics we are discussing. Please remember that assessments are powerful tools if you are honest with yourself. Take your time and be truthful in your responses so that your results are an honest reflection of you. Your level of commitment in completing the assessments honestly will determine how much you learn about yourself."*

Allow participants to turn to the first page of their assessment and read the instructions silently to themselves. Then tell them: *"All of the assessments have similar formats, but they have different scales, responses, scoring instructions and methods for interpretation. If you do not understand how to complete the assessment, ask me before you turn the page to begin."*

Then tell them: *"Because there is no time limit for completing the assessments, take your time and work at your own pace. Do not answer the assessments as you think others would like you to answer them or how you think others see you. These assessments are for you to reflect on your life and explore some of the barriers that are keeping you from living a more satisfying life. Before completing each assessment, be sure to read the instructions."*

Make sure that nobody has a question, then tell them, *"Learning about yourself can be a positive and motivating experience. Don't stress about taking the assessments or discovering your results. Just respond honestly and learn as much about yourself as you can."*

Tell participants to turn the page and begin answering with Question 1. Allow sufficient time for all participants to complete the assessment. Answer any questions people have. As people begin to finish, read through the instructions for scoring the assessment. Have participants begin to score their own assessment and transfer their scores for interpretation. Make sure that nobody has a question about how to do the scoring.

Review the purpose of the interpretation table included after each assessment. Tell the participants: *"Remember, this assessment was not designed to label you. Rather, it was designed to develop a baseline of your behaviors. Regardless of how you score on an assessment, consider it a starting point upon which you can develop healthier habits. Take your time, reflect on your results, and note how they compare to what you already know about yourself."*

After participants have completed, scored, and interpreted their assessment, facilitators can use the self-exploration activities included in each module to supplement their traditional tools and techniques to help participants function more effectively.

(Continued on the next page)

Managing Trauma Workbook

Format of the Managing Trauma Workbook (Continued)

Self-Exploration Activities

This workbook will provide self-exploration activities that can be used to manage trauma issues. These activities, included after each of the assessments, will prompt self-reflection and promote self-understanding. They use a variety of formats to accommodate all learning styles, foster introspection, and promote pro-social behaviors, life skills and coping skills. The activities in each module correlate to the assessments to enable you to identify and select activities quickly and easily.

Self-exploration activities assist participants in self-reflection, enhance self-knowledge, identify potential ineffective behaviors, and teach more effective ways of coping with irrational behaviors. They are is designed to help participants make a series of discoveries that lead to increased social and emotional competencies, as well as to serve as an energizing way to help participants grow personally and professionally. These brief, easy-to-use self-reflection tools are designed to promote insight and self-growth.

Many different types of guided self-exploration activities are provided for you to pick and choose the activities that are most needed by your participants and the ones that will be most appealing to them. The unique features of the exploration activities make them user-friendly and appropriate for a variety of individual sessions and group sessions.

In these activities, participants will have a variety of opportunities:

- To explore how they could make changes in their lives to feel better. These activities are designed to help participants reflect on their current life situations, discover new ways of living more effectively, and implement changes in their lives to accommodate these changes.

- To journal as a way of enhancing their self-awareness. Through journaling prompts, participants will be able to write about the thoughts, attitudes, feelings, and behaviors that have contributed to, or are currently contributing to, their current life situation. Through journaling, participants are able to safely address their concerns, hopes and dreams for the future.

- To explore their reactions to trauma by examining their past for negative patterns and learning new ways of dealing more effectively in the future. These activities are designed to help participants reflect on their lives in ways that will allow them to develop healthier lifestyles.

Introduction

The Stigma Awareness Approach

It is important that facilitators keep an open mind about mental health issues and the stigma attached to people experiencing these issues. Rather than thinking of people as having a mental disorder, or being mentally ill, the *Erasing the Stigma of Mental Health Issues through Awareness* series is designed to help facilitators to diminish the stigma that surrounds people suffering from unwanted thoughts, feelings and actions issues. Stigmas occur when people are unduly labeled, which sets the stage for discrimination and humiliation. Facilitators are able to help to erase the stigma of mental illness through enhanced awareness of the factors that activate the issues, accentuate the depth of the issues, and accelerate awareness and understanding.

To assist you, a module titled *Erasing the Stigma of Mental Health Issues* is included to provide activities for helping to erase the stigma associated with unwanted thoughts, feelings and actions issues.

The Awareness Modules

The reproducible awareness modules contained in this workbook will help you identify and select assessments and activities easily and quickly:

Module I: The Story of My Trauma
   This module will help participants share all aspects of their story in a safe way and put it into a positive perspective.

Module II: My Escape-Mode
   This module will help participants explore the various ways that they avoid and numb to forget their traumatic experience, and provides tools for coping with these symptoms.

Module III: Managing My Transition Experiences
   This module will help participants explore ways that they can effectively manage trauma and move on from their traumatic experience.

Module IV: Tools for Coping with My Symptoms
   This module will help participants explore the various ways that they re-experience their trauma and provides tools for coping with these symptoms.

Module V: Erasing the Stigma of Mental Health Issues
   This module will help participants explore the stigma of having experienced a traumatic event in their lives and the impact that the stigma has on them.

Our thanks to these professionals who make us look good!

Art Director - Joy Dey

Assistant Art Director – Mathew Pawlak

Editorial Director - Carlene Sippola

Editor - Eileen Regen, M.ED., CJE - Lifelong Teacher

Reviewer - Carol Butler, MS Ed, RN, C – Skills Expert

Reviewer – Nadine Hartig, Ph.D., LPC, LCSW - Trauma Counselor

Reviewer - Jay Leutenberg, CASA – Proofreader Extraordinaire

Managing Trauma Workbook

Table of Contents

Module I – The Story of My Trauma 17
Skills Emphasized in Each Activity Handout 18
The Story of My Trauma Scale Introduction and Directions 19
The Story of My Trauma Scale Scoring Directions 21
Profile Interpretation 21
Scale Descriptions 21
My Story 22
Thoughts about My Trauma 23-27
Me – Before My Trauma 28
What I Was Like Before My Trauma 29
Who I Am Now 30
My View of the World 31

Module II – My Escape-Mode 33
Skills Emphasized in Each Activity Handout 34
My Escape-Mode Scale Introduction and Directions 35
Coping with Avoiding and Numbing Symptoms Scale 36
Scoring Directions 37
Profile Interpretation 37
Scale Descriptions 37
Avoiding Places 38
Avoiding People 39
Avoiding Situations 40
Suppressing My Feelings 41
Feeling Those Feelings 42
Avoiding My Feelings? 43
Picturing My Fear 44
I Feel Guilty! 45
Who Created the Trauma? 46
Expressing Feelings 47
Escaping through Addiction 48
Ways I Shut Down 49
Spacing Out 50
Ways I Self-Harm 51
Alternatives to Self-Harm 52

Table of Contents

Module III – Managing My Transition Experiences 53
- *Skills* Emphasized in Each Activity Handout 54
- Managing My Transition Experiences Introduction and Directions 55
- Managing My Transition Experiences Scale............................. 56
- Scoring Directions 57
- Profile Interpretation 57
- Scale Descriptions... 57
- Intimate Relationships 58
- Connected or Not 59
- Trust.. 60
- My View of Others... 61
- Physical Boundaries 62
- My Safety Plan 63
- Physical Safety 64
- Environmental Safety 65
- Emotional Safety.. 66
- A Safety Contract 67
- My Safe Places 68
- Victim Thinking 69
- A Historical Perspective 70
- My Angry Moments 71
- Constructive Vs. Destructive Anger Management...................... 72
- Why am I so Angry?.. 73
- Hopefulness 74
- Self-Esteem 75
- My Strengths and My Talents 76
- Rewriting Your Narrative... 77
- Solving My Problem 78
- My Life Purpose 79
- Add Life Structure... 80

Table of Contents

Module IV – Tools for Coping with My Symptoms 81
   Skills Emphasized in Each Activity Handout 82
   Tools for Coping with My Symptoms Introduction and Directions 83
   Tools for Coping with My Symptoms Scale 84
   Scoring Directions 85
   Profile Interpretation 85
   Scale Descriptions 85
   Intrusive Thoughts 86
   My Trauma Triggers 87
   Trigger Management 88
   My Nightmare and My Trauma 89
   The Value of Positive Distractions 90
   Flashbacks 91
   My Sleep Patterns 92
   Tracking My Sleep Patterns 93
   Sleep Tips 94
   Jittery, Anxious? Edgy? Jumpy? Agitated? Worried? Scared? Skittish? 95
   Over-Cautious? 96
   Problem Solving for the Over-Cautious 97
   Anticipating High-Risk Situations 98
   Coping: Let's Meditate 99
   Coping: Deep Breathing 100
   Coping: Mindfulness and Paying Attention 101
   Coping: Total Body Relaxation 102
   Ways to Make Meaning 103

Table of Contents

Module V – Erasing the Stigma of Mental Health Issues 105
   Skills Emphasized in Each Activity Handout 106
   Erasing the Stigma of Mental Health Issues Introduction. 107
   Two Types of Mental Health Stigma 108
   The Stigma of Trauma – THE PAST 109
   The Stigma of Trauma – THE PRESENT 110
   Speak Your Mind 111
   If We Stamp Out the Stigma … 112
   Glenn Close said … 113
   Effects of Trauma Issues 114
   The Stigma of Going to a Mental Health Therapist 115
   Stereotypes 116
   Will You Speak Out? 117
   My Negative Thoughts 118
   Focus on Your Strengths 119
   Ways I Try to Minimize My Trauma Stress 120
   Ways I am Treated 121
   Self-Doubt 122
   A Poster about the STIGMA of People Who
      Have Experienced a Trauma 123
   A Poster about ACCEPTANCE of People Who Have
      Experienced a Trauma 124
   DE-STIGMA-TIZE with the Facts about Mental Health Issues 125
   Coping with the Stigma of a Mental Health Issue 126
   Speak Out Against Stigmas 127

MODULE I

The Story of My Trauma

There is no greater agony than bearing an untold story inside of you.

~ Maya Angelou

Name _____

Date _____

Managing Trauma Workbook

Module I – The Story of My Trauma
Skills Emphasized in Each Activity Handout

My Story .... page 22
    Tell one's story by journaling details about the trauma.

Thoughts about My Trauma .... page 23
    Clarify aspects of the trauma by responding to 15 questions.

Me – Before My Trauma .... page 28
    Show self-identity specifics by depicting and describing oneself before the trauma.

What I Was Like Before My Trauma .... page 29
    Define one's characteristics before the trauma by responding to five questions.

Who I Am Now .... page 30
    Compare one's sense of self after the trauma by answering the same five questions about current traits.

My View of the World .... page 31
    Share views of one's world by completing five sentences.

The Story of My Trauma Scale
Introduction and Directions

It is important to explore what one has experienced in an atmosphere of feeling safe, not re-experiencing the trauma or feeling overwhelmed. Therefore it is important to tell your story safely and begin to integrate aspects of your traumatic event into your overall identity. To begin to tell and understand your story, it will help to explore your experience, self-identity and trauma triggers.

This scale contains 18 statements designed to help you explore the various aspects that surround your trauma story. Read each of the statements and decide whether the statement describes you or not. If the statement does describe you, circle the number in the YES column next to that item. If the statement does not describe you, circle the number in the NO column next to that item. Do not worry about the numbers for now.

In the following example, the circled 2 indicates the statement does describe the person completing the inventory:

About my trauma event ...

	YES	NO
1. I have shared the story of my trauma with important people in my life.	(2)	1

This is not a test. Since there are no right or wrong answers, do not spend too much time thinking about your answers. Be sure to respond to every statement.

(Turn to the next page and begin.)

Managing Trauma Workbook

The Story of My Trauma Scale

About my trauma event …

	YES	NO
1. I have shared the story of my trauma with important people in my life	2	1
2. I often think about my traumatic event	2	1
3. I understand how the traumatic event has had an impact on me	2	1
4. I can't make sense of why it had to happen	1	2
5. I am traumatized all over again when I re-experience the event	1	2
6. I don't want to think about the event	1	2

SCALE I = _____

7. I don't recognize the person I am anymore	1	2
8. I still see the world as a positive place	2	1
9. I feel guilty, ashamed and/or embarrassed about what happened	1	2
10. I feel good about myself even though the event happened	2	1
11. I have become isolated and withdrawn	1	2
12. I believe I am damaged	1	2

SCALE II = _____

13. I cannot seem to anticipate what will trigger my memories	1	2
14. I feel prepared when I encounter a trigger of the event	2	1
15. I never know when something will trigger the event	1	2
16. I have a plan for when I begin to feel stressed about the event	2	1
17. I know the situations that are challenging for me	2	1
18. Many sights and sounds trigger a re-occurrence of my trauma	1	2

SCALE III = _____

Go to the Scoring Directions

The Story of My Trauma

The Story of My Trauma Scale
Scoring Directions

The Story of My Trauma Scale you just completed is designed to measure your readiness to tell your trauma story. For each of the sections on the previous page, count the scores you circled. Put that total on the line marked TOTAL at the end of each section.

Then, transfer your total to the space below:

I. **My Experience** = _____

II. **My Self-Identity Total** = _____

III. **My Triggers Total** = _____

Add your scores together for your Grand Total. _____

Profile Interpretation

Individual Score	Grand Total	Result	Indications
6 - 7	18 - 23	Low	Low scores indicate that you have not accepted and integrated the traumatic event into your life.
8 - 10	24 - 30	Moderate	Moderate scores indicate that you have somewhat accepted and integrated the traumatic event into your life.
11 - 12	31 - 36	High	High scores indicate that you have accepted and integrated the traumatic event into your life.

Scale Descriptions

I. **My Experience** – People scoring High on this scale have made sense of the trauma they experienced, shared their story to others in an open, honest and direct way, and integrated their trauma into other life experiences.

II. **My Self-Identity** – People scoring High on this scale have a positive view of themselves and the world in general. They do not feel guilty, ashamed or embarrassed about what happened to them and they feel good about themselves.

III. **My Triggers** – People scoring High on this scale are aware of their trauma triggers and have explored and integrated ways to manage these triggers in their lives.

GRAND TOTAL – High scores on all three scales indicate that the person is aware of the impact of their trauma on their life and has made strides to integrate the traumatic event with current daily experiences. The following pages will be helpful to everyone, no matter how they scored.

Managing Trauma Workbook

My Story

Telling one's story is healing! Many people who experience trauma feel guilty, ashamed or embarrassed to tell anyone their story. A great way to tell your story safely is by writing it out.

In the space that follows, write about the trauma that you experienced in as much detail as possible. Use the back of this page if you need additional space.

The Story of My Trauma

Thoughts about My Trauma - PAGE 1

Think about the trauma you experienced.
Journaling about that experience can help you make meaning of the event and reduce your distress.

Below, journal about your trauma.

When did the event happen? _____
_____

What was happening before the event? _____
_____
_____
_____
_____
_____
_____

Did you feel that something was not right? _____
_____

If so, explain your feelings. _____
_____
_____
_____
_____
_____
_____

(Continued on the next page)

Thoughts about My Trauma - PAGE 2

What do you remember about the event (sights, smells, sounds, feelings, thoughts)?

_____
_____
_____
_____
_____
_____
_____
_____
_____
_____
_____
_____
_____
_____
_____
_____

How did you know it was over? _____
_____
_____
_____
_____
_____

(Continued on the next page)

Thoughts about My Trauma - PAGE 3

What did you do after it was over? _____

_____

_____

_____

_____

_____

_____

_____

_____

_____

_____

_____

_____

_____

_____

_____

_____

_____

_____

In what ways has the event changed your life? _____

_____

_____

_____

_____

_____

_____

_____

(Continued on the next page)

Thoughts about My Trauma - *PAGE 4*

In what ways has the event changd your relationships with significant others/partners?

_____
_____
_____
_____
_____
_____
_____
_____
_____

In what ways has the event changed your relationships with family?

_____
_____
_____
_____
_____
_____
_____
_____
_____

In what ways has the event changed your relationships with friends?

_____
_____
_____
_____
_____
_____
_____

(Continued on the next page)

Thoughts about My Trauma - *PAGE 5*

How has the event affected your future, in a negative way?

_____
_____
_____
_____
_____
_____
_____
_____
_____
_____
_____
_____

In what ways has the event changed your relationships with friends?

_____
_____
_____
_____
_____
_____
_____
_____
_____
_____
_____
_____

Managing Trauma Workbook

Me - Before My Trauma

Your self-identity can change as the result of a trauma.
It can help you to explore the way you were before the trauma.

In the space that follows, draw, doodle, write about or list words and phrases that describe who you were before your trauma.

What parts of your identity seem to be missing since the traumatic event?

_____

_____

The Story of My Trauma

What I Was Like Before My Trauma

Think about yourself before you experienced the traumatic event. What were you like?

Answer the following questions to get a more comprehensive sense of who you were.

In what were you interested before the trauma?

___

___

___

What made you happy before the trauma?

___

___

___

What made you sad before the trauma?

___

___

___

What did you like most about yourself before the trauma?

___

___

___

What were your dreams before the trauma?

___

___

___

Managing Trauma Workbook

Who I Am Now

Think about yourself after you experienced a traumatic event. What are you like now?

Answer the following questions to get a more comprehensive sense of who you are now.

In what are you interested now?

_____
_____
_____

What makes you happy now?

_____
_____
_____

What makes you sad now?

_____
_____
_____

What do you like most about yourself now?

_____
_____
_____

What are your dreams now?

_____
_____
_____

The Story of My Trauma

My View of My World

Experiencing a traumatic event can definitely change the way people view the world in general.

In the space that follows, describe how you now view your world.

I believe the world is a _____ place because
_____
_____
_____

The thing in this world I care most about is _____
_____
_____
_____
_____

Through my negative actions, I can affect my environment by _____
_____
_____
_____
_____

Through my positive actions, I can affect my environment by _____
_____
_____
_____
_____

My life would be better if I could _____
_____
_____
_____
_____

MODULE II

My Escape-Mode

You will find peace not be trying to escape your problems but by confronting them courageously.

~ J. Donald Walters

Name _____

Date _____

Module II – My Escape-Mode
Skills Emphasized in Each Activity Handout

Avoiding Places .... page 38
Identify four places one avoids, the associated memories, and how one is hindered by the avoidance. Differentiate between the easiest and most difficult to avoid and identify reasons.

Avoiding People .... page 39
Identify four people one avoids, the associated memories, and how one is hindered by the avoidance. Differentiate between the easiest and most difficult to avoid and identify reasons.

Avoiding Situations .... page 40
Identify four situations one avoids, the associated memories, and how one is hindered by the avoidance. Differentiate between the easiest and most difficult and identify reasons.

Suppressing My Feelings .... page 41
Demonstrate insight into emotional numbness by completing seven sentence-starters related to suppressed feelings. Personalize a quotation about the danger of suppressing and benefits of expressing feelings.

Feeling Those Feelings .... page 42
Select the most descriptive term for one's basic four emotions. State when and where the feelings occur.

Avoiding My Feelings? .... page 43
Identify five or more ways one avoids feelings, what is avoided and the effects. Provide an example to illustrate a reason for the avoidance.

Picturing My Fear .... page 44
Imagine and depict one's fear then draw how one would like the fear to appear. State ways to reduce the fear.

I Feel Guilty! .... page 45
Rate the intensity of one's guilt on a ten point scale. Demonstrate insight by responding to five questions about one's role in the traumatic event.

Who Created the Trauma? .... page 46
Identify four people who contributed to or created the trauma. Share how one was hurt, feelings toward the people and the steps one can take to let go of the negative feelings and/or forgive.

Expressing Feelings .... page 47
Express eight negative emotions and their positive counterparts by completing fourteen insight-oriented sentence starters.

Escaping through Addictions .... page 48
Identify five ways one may try to numb oneself through addictive behaviors and the detrimental effects. Document five or more healthy alternatives. State which one wants to stop the most and steps to take.

Ways I Shut Down .... page 49
Identify six or more ways one shuts down and the negative and positive effects on oneself and relationships. Describe how one can stop shutting down.

Zoning Out .... page 50
Elaborate about nine or more avoidant activities and the time spent on them. Describe nine or more healthy alternative diversions.

Ways I Self-Harm .... page 51
Select which self-harm actions one employs from among ten possibilities. Rank one's top three and state when they are used.

Alternatives to Self-Harm .... page 52
Depict positive ways to feel alive – healthy and productive alternatives to self-harm, by creating a photo gallery of drawings, doodles and other images.

My Escape-Mode Scale
Introduction and Directions

People who have experienced a traumatic event attempt to protect themselves from the intense emotions involved in the event by escaping: avoiding, becoming emotionally numb and tuning out of the present.

Many people will attempt to avoid dealing with their traumatic experience by trying to avoid everything associated with the event including the following:
- Avoiding people, places and situations
- Numbing by emotionally escaping the present situation

This scale contains 30 statements designed to help you explore how much you try to avoid dealing with the trauma you experienced. Choose your most traumatic situation and briefly write it on the line at the top of the page. Read each of the statements and decide whether the statement describes you or not. If the statement does describe you, circle the number in the YES column next to that item. If the statement does not describe you, circle the number in the NO column next to that item.

In the following example, the circled 2 indicates the statement does describe the person completing the inventory

	Yes	No
I try to ignore my memories and hope they'll go away.	(2)	1

This is not a test. Since there are no right or wrong answers, do not spend too much time thinking about your answers. Be sure to respond to every statement.

(Turn to the next page and begin.)

Managing Trauma Workbook

My Escape-Mode Scale

My Traumatic Situation _____

	YES	NO
I try to ignore my memories and hope they'll go away	2	1
I have disowned the event	2	1
I can't face the trauma	2	1
It hurts too much to process the memories	2	1
I want the memories to go away	2	1
I avoid anything that reminds me of the trauma	2	1
I avoid places that remind me of the trauma	2	1
I don't want to recall details of the trauma	2	1
I don't leave the house for fear of similar situations	2	1
I cannot connect with anyone who was part of the trauma	2	1
I feel guilty about the event and avoid discussing it	2	1
I avoid engaging with anyone who wants to talk about it	2	1
I avoid anything that reminds me of the trauma	2	1
I use substances to avoid my thoughts	2	1
I use my addiction to avoid my thoughts	2	1

A. Total = _____

	YES	NO
I have shut down emotionally	2	1
I'm afraid of being overwhelmed by my feelings	2	1
I can't feel anything	2	1
I feel embarrassed about the event	2	1
I feel detached from others	2	1
I often find it difficult to concentrate	2	1
I harm myself to feel alive	2	1
I isolate myself	2	1
I act like a robot without feelings	2	1
I daydream a lot to escape life	2	1
I want to sleep a lot to escape my life	2	1
I often feel separate from my body	2	1
I only remember certain aspects of my trauma	2	1
I avoid places that remind me of the trauma	2	1
I feel numb in certain situations	2	1

N. Total = _____

Go to the Scoring Directions

My Escape-Mode Scale
Scoring Directions

The *My Escape-Mode Scale* you just completed is designed to measure how much you attempt to avoid remembering your traumatic experience, and how you numb yourself and your feelings. For both of the sections on the previous page, count the scores you circled.
Put that total on the line marked TOTAL at the end of each section.

Then, transfer your total to the space below:

        A. = AVOIDING   TOTAL _____

        N. = NUMBING   TOTAL _____

Add your scores together for your Grand Total. _____

Profile Interpretation

Individual Score	Grand Total	Result	Indications
15-19	30 - 39	Low	Low scores indicate that you do not seem to avoid and numb your symptoms.
20-25	40 - 51	Moderate	Moderate scores indicate that you sometimes seem to avoid and numb your symptoms.
26 - 30	52 - 60	High	High scores indicate that you often seem to avoid and numb your symptoms.

Scale Descriptions

A. AVOIDING – People scoring high on this scale tend to ignore their trauma, and ultimately avoid people, places, and situations that are reminders.

N. NUMBING – People scoring high on this scale attempt to numb themselves with the use of illegal substances, harming themselves and daydreaming, as well as being unable to deal with their feelings effectively.

GRAND TOTAL – High scores on both scales indicate that the person uses numbing and avoiding as a way of not dealing with intrusive memories, flashbacks, and feelings associated with having experienced a trauma. The following activities will be helpful to everyone, no matter how they scored.

Managing Trauma Workbook

Avoiding Places

People often want to forget and stop re-experiencing their traumatic event. This is a natural reaction. If that is true of you, you are probably spending a lot of your life avoiding places that remind you of the trauma.

Answer the following questions to identify how much effort you are exerting to avoid the places that would bring back memories of your trauma.

A Place I Avoid	What This Place Reminds Me of	What I Miss by Avoiding This Place
EXAMPLE: Traveling to other countries.	The setting of my traumatic event was out of my country.	I love to travel, and I have always wanted to see some other countries.

Which places are the easiest to avoid? When is it most difficult? Why? _____
_____
_____

My Escape-Mode

Avoiding People

People often want to forget and stop re-experiencing their traumatic event. This is a natural reaction. If that is true of you, you are probably spending a lot of your life avoiding people that remind you of the trauma.

Answer the following questions to identify how much effort you are exerting to avoid the people that would bring back memories of your trauma.

A Person I Avoid and This Person's Relationship to Me	What This Person Reminds Me Of	What I Miss by Avoiding This Person
EXAMPLE: Sam, my son's friend	My son used Sam's gun to die by suicide.	I care about Sam and miss seeing him. It wasn't his fault.

Which people are the easiest to avoid? Why? _____
_____
_____

Which are the most difficult? Why? _____
_____
_____

Managing Trauma Workbook

Avoiding Situations

People often want to forget and stop re-experiencing their traumatic event. This is a natural reaction. If that is true of you, you are probably spending a lot of your life avoiding situations that remind you of the trauma.

Answer the following questions to identify how much effort you are exerting to avoid the situations that would bring back memories of your trauma.

A Situation I Avoid	What This Situation Reminds Me Of	What I Miss by Avoiding This Situation
EXAMPLE: Going to my local market.	I was there when a robbery occurred. It was very frightening.	It is the only market for miles and their food is excellent.

Which situation is the easiest to avoid? Why? _____

_____

_____

Which situation is the most difficult? Why? _____

_____

_____

My Escape-Mode

Suppressing My Feelings

Sometimes it is easier for the victims of traumatic events to simply try to suppress their feelings so that they don't have to feel them anymore; they become emotionally numb.

For the following activity, answer each of the sentence starters below.

I suppress such feelings as…..

The feelings I have and enjoy include…...

The feelings I am no longer able to feel include…..

The feelings I think I no longer deserve to feel include…..

The feelings I am embarrassed to feel include…..

The feelings I am ashamed to feel include…..

The feelings I do not feel safe expressing include…..

> *We all know that being able to express deep emotion can literally save a person's life, and suppressing emotion can kill you both spiritually and physically.*
>
> *~ Lisa Kleypas*

Managing Trauma Workbook

Feeling those Feelings

People who have experienced a traumatic event often try to avoid their feelings
An important strategy is to identify the emotions you feel. Below are four basic feelings. There are many facets of each feeling.

Look at the listings of feelings and add your own to identify which degree of the emotion you feel.

You Become Angry – Annoyed, Bitter, Furious, Outraged, Hostile, Enraged, Mad

Which of these do you feel the most? When do you experience the feeling? Where are you?

_____

_____

_____

You Feel Glad – Caring, Calm, Relaxed, Content, Fulfilled, Delighted, Loved, Peaceful

Which of these do you feel the most? When do you experience the feeling? Where are you?

_____

_____

_____

You are Sad – Helpless, Pessimistic, Useless, Depressed, Miserable, Hurt, Disappointed

Which of these do you feel the most? When do you experience the feeling? Where are you?

_____

_____

_____

You Become Scared – Vulnerable, Terrified, Devastated, Fearful, Victimized, Frantic

Which of these do you feel the most? When do you experience the feeling? Where are you?

_____

_____

My Escape-Mode

Avoiding My Feelings?

People who have experienced very painful emotions try to control their pain by shutting off their emotions.

Think about how you avoid your feelings, what you avoid and the effects this avoidance has on you.

Ways I Avoid My Feelings	What I Avoid	The Effect this Has on Me
Example: *I stay away from places that might trigger feelings.*	*I avoid small grocery stores that remind me of the traumatic event.*	*I can shop for groceries only at large stores that are more crowded.*
I stay away from places that might trigger feelings.		
I stay away from people that might trigger feelings.		
I try not to think of memories that bring back my feelings.		
I try to stay numb.		
I am not comfortable feeling anymore.		
Other		

Why do you think you avoid your feelings? Give an example. _____

_____

_____

Managing Trauma Workbook

Picturing My Fear

Many people feel afraid after they have experienced a trauma.
Some may have panic attacks.

One way to gain control over your fear and/or panic is to use your imagination and draw a picture or a caricature of what your fear and/or panic attack looks like to you.

Is the picture as fearful as you think it is? How can you reduce your fearful feelings?

_____

_____

_____

On the other side of the page, draw what you'd like your fear or panic to look like.

My Escape-Mode

I Feel Guilty!

Guilt occurs when you feel bad after something that has happened, whether you were an active participant or not. Even though they may not have had a part in the trauma they experienced (or even if they did), some people feel guilty after a traumatic event.

Answer the questions below to explore your level of guilt.

My level of guilt about what happened to me (place an X on the line below):

Not Very Guilty **Very Guilty**
0--10

What was your part in the traumatic event?

_____
_____
_____

What do you feel guilty about?

_____
_____
_____

Why did you chose to handle the situation like you did?

_____
_____
_____

What would you do differently?

_____
_____
_____

Is your guilt realistic and/or justifiable? Explain_____

_____
_____

Managing Trauma Workbook

Who Created the Trauma?

It is important to explore the feelings you have about the creator of the trauma that has become an issue to you.

In this table identify those people who you believe created, or helped to create, your trauma(s). This may be one person or several people; someone whose name you know or do not know; a country; a leader; a group.

My Trauma _____

People Who Have Created the Trauma	How These People Hurt Me	Feelings about Those People
Example: My Kidnapper	He stole my faith in people, and now I am afraid to go out of the house.	Hate, fear, sadness
Example: People who caused a riot at a rally.	It scared me so much I don't want to go out in a crowd.	I admire them for feeling so passionately about their cause. I just wish they had done it peacefully.

What steps can you take to let go of your negative feelings and/or forgive?
(That does not necessarily mean *forget*.)

_____

_____

_____

My Escape-Mode

Expressing Feelings

Some people are unable to express feelings as they are unable to find words to describe their feelings. When you are able to express positive and negative feelings, you will find that you become more content with your own feelings and can experience them easier.

Finish the following sentence starters.

I'm very sad about	I feel good about
I am very frightened about	I feel safe when
I feel defeated when	I feel uplifted when
I feel anxious when	I am calm when
I feel very uncomfortable when	I am comfortable when
I feel hopeless when	I feel hopeful when
I am optimistic when	I am pessimistic when
(other) I …	(other) I …

Escaping through Addictions

Some people, in an attempt to numb themselves from the traumatic event they experienced, use stimulants and substances, and indulge in addictive behaviors.

In the spaces that follow, identify the various substances and addictive behaviors that you use to numb yourself.

My Substances and/or Addictions	How this Numbs Me	How this Negatively Affects My Life	What I Could do Instead
Example: Gambling	It distracts me. I look forward to it. I do not think about my trauma at all.	I seldom win and my family needs the money that I lose. It causes huge arguments in our household.	I could start woodworking again. It will distract me and I can build some things we need in the house rather than buy them.

Which of the substances or addictive behaviors that you use to numb yourself would you like to stop? What steps can you take to stop using or doing this altogether?

_____

_____

_____

My Escape-Mode

Ways I Shut Down

Trauma survivors will do what they can to avoid being in situations and relationships that might trigger the traumatic event. Thus, they shut down or numb themselves.

Think about the ways you do this in your life.

Ways I Shut Down	How this Affects Me and/or My Relationships in a POSITIVE Way	How this Affects Me and/or My Relationships in a NEGATIVE Way
Retreat from Life		
Detach from People		
Stare off into Space		
Act on Autopilot		
Separate my Mind from my Body		
Feel Apathetic		
Other		

How can you stop shutting down? _____
_____
_____

Managing Trauma Workbook

Zoning Out

Trauma survivors often find ways to protect themselves from traumatic events by zoning out to avoid thinking about the event.

What are some of the ways you zone out to avoid thinking about the trauma you have experienced.

Ways I Zone Out	Length of Time I Do This	What I Believe This Does for Me	Is it Healthy for Me or Not? Why?
Watch television			
Daydream			
Go to a fantasy world			
Use social media			
Play video games			
Participate in high-risk activities			
Abuse substances and/or develop addictions			
Read a spell-binding book			
Go out with Friends			
Other			
Other			

My Escape-Mode

Ways I Self-Harm

Many people who have experienced trauma in their lives will attempt to express their feelings by harming themselves. Which of the following do you do to harm yourself?

Place a check in the box in front of those that apply to you, and describe what you do.

You do not need to share this page. Be honest with yourself!

☐ I overeat
_____

☐ I take excessive risks
_____

☐ I cut myself
_____

☐ I use alcohol to excess
_____

☐ I smoke
_____

☐ I spend money excessively
_____

☐ I put myself in risky situations
_____

☐ I use illegal substances to excess
_____

☐ I remain in a harmful relationship
_____

☐ I have an addiction
_____

Rank your top three self-harmful behaviors and when you use them:

1) _____
2) _____
3) _____

Managing Trauma Workbook

Alternatives to Self-Harm

People often harm themselves to feel alive.

Prepare a photo gallery of alternatives to self-harm (funny movie, a hobby or craft cut outs, therapist and person, etc.). This photo gallery can include newspaper or magazine cutouts, drawings, doodles, or images from online photo.

MODULE III

Managing My Transition Experiences

A lot of people resist transition and therefore never allow themselves to enjoy who they are.

~ Nikki Giovanni

Name _____

Date _____

Managing Trauma Workbook

Module III – Managing My Transition Experiences
Skills Emphasized in Each Activity Handout

Intimate Relationships ....page 58
  Demonstrate insight about six aspects of intimate relations by completing sentence starters.

Connected or Not? ....page 59
  Document levels of connectedness with significant people, and the reasons.

Trust ....page 60
  Discuss trust and disclosure issues related to the trauma.

My View of Others ....page 61
  Depict and describe one's view of significant people in one's life.

Physical Boundaries...page 62
  Describe six aspects of personal space boundaries.

My Safety Plan..page 63
  Identify four helpful people, five safety suggestions used, and other safeguards.

Physical Safety...page 64
  State ways to improve safety in five specified places, plus other locales.

Environmental Safety ....page 65
  Describe ways to implement five safety suggestions.

Emotional Safety ....page 66
  List five people isolated from, reasons, and ways to re-connect.

A Safety Contract ....page 67
  Contract for safety re: four types of self-harm, and when to seek help.

My Safe Places...page 68
  Draw and tell about four safe places, the most treasured, and why.

Victim Thinking...page 69
  Identify signs of victim thinking from sixteen prompts. Post nine affirmations.

A Historical Perspective ....page 70
  Imagine an admired person's perspective of one's trauma and ways to use the wisdom.

My Angry Moments...page 71
  Share four anger experiences and ways to express feelings appropriately.

Constructive Vs. Destructive Anger Management ....page 72
  Compare destructive and constructive ways one manages anger.

Why am I so Angry? ....page 73
  Demonstrate insight into anger by responding to seven questions.

Hopefulness..page 74
  Demonstrate hope through six sentence completions. Personalize an inspirational quote.

Self-Esteem ....page 75
  Elaborate on four categories of one's positive qualities. Share resultant insights.

My Strengths and Talents ....page 76
  List five strengths, talents and positive personality traits; note ways the trauma improved these.

Re-Writing Your Narrative ....page 77
  Describe the traumatic event with oneself as hero/heroine and note the feasibility of that role.

Solving My Problem ....page 78
  Complete and document more than ten problem solving steps.

My Life Purpose ....page 79
  Describe five aspects of own purpose.

Add Life Structure ....page 80
  Describe one's primary trigger; state ways to decrease related triggers in six areas of one's life.

Managing My Transition Experiences Scale
Introduction and Directions

Experiencing a traumatic event can, and probably has, changed you in a variety of ways. It is important that you accept what has happened to you, integrate the experience into your life, look to the future and seek growth and opportunities.

This scale contains 30 statements designed to help you explore how ready you are to make a transition to a better future.

Read each item carefully and decide how much the statement describes you. In each of the choices listed, circle the number of your response.

In the following example, the circled number under 1 indicates the statement is True for the person completing the inventory.

	True	NOT True
1. I no longer have compassion for others	(1)	2

This is not a test and there are no right or wrong answers. Do not spend too much time thinking about your answers. Your initial response will be the most true for you. Be sure to respond to every statement.

(Turn to the next page and begin.)

Managing My Transition Experiences Scale

	True	NOT True
1. I no longer have compassion for others	1	2
2. I want to have healthy relationships	2	1
3. I avoid getting too intimate	1	2
4. I still appreciate some people	2	1
5. I don't care about other people anymore	1	2
6. I don't feel as if I can trust anyone again	1	2

SCALE I = _____

7. I don't feel safe	1	2
8. I have a safety plan	2	1
9. I feel as if someone might harm me	1	2
10. I am careful of my environment	2	1
11. I am afraid I will harm myself	1	2
12. I have an effective system for solving problems	2	1

SCALE II = _____

13. I have lost interest in life	1	2
14. I can often envision a happy future for myself	2	1
15. I feel hopeless	1	2
16. I am too stressed about my trauma to enjoy life	1	2
17. I feel as if I have limited control over my future	1	2
18. I am hopeful to have many good things happen in my life	2	1

SCALE III = _____

19. I can control my emotions	2	1
20. I experience angry outbursts	1	2
21. I get annoyed easily	1	2
22. I know techniques for managing my anger	2	1
23. I often experience moments of rage	1	2
24. I say things out of anger that I am sorry for later	1	2

SCALE IV = _____

Go to the Scoring Directions

Managing My Transition Experiences Scale
Scoring Directions

The *Managing My Transition Experiences Scale* is designed to help you explore how ready you are to move on and make the transition to a new life. On the self-assessment page, add the numbers that you circled in each section and write the scores on each of the TOTAL lines. You will receive a total in the range from 6 to 12. Then, transfer those numbers to the space below.

Scale I: Positive Relationships = _____

Scale II: Feeling Safe = _____

Scale III: Overcoming Hopelessnes = _____

Scale IV: Managing Anger = _____

Profile Interpretation

Individual Score	Result	Indications
6 - 7	Low	If you scored in the LOW range, you are not ready to move on from the traumatic event you experienced.
8 - 10	Moderate	If you scored in the MODERATE range, you are fairly ready to move on from the traumatic event you experienced.
11 - 12	High	If you scored in the HIGH range, you are ready to move on from the traumatic event you experienced.

Scale Descriptions

I **Positive Relationships** – People scoring high on this scale still care about people, trust others, and want to have intimate relationships in their lives.

II **Feeling Safe** – People scoring high on this scale have a safety plan in place, are not a threat to harm themselves, and do not fear others.

III **Overcoming Hopelessness** – People scoring high on this scale are interested in life, expect positive things to happen to them, and plan to have a great future.

IV **Managing Anger** – People scoring high on this scale are able to control their emotions, especially angry outbursts.

Intimate Relationships

In order to move on from traumatic events it is important to maintain intimate relationships. Often, people who have experienced a trauma find it difficult to develop and maintain intimate relationships.

If any of these questions do not apply to you, explain.

I am uncomfortable disclosing personal information about myself because …

Since my trauma I've not been able to have an intimate relationship because …

I must get to know people before I can trust them because …

I've had a difficult time being in a sexual relationship because …

Other people do not fulfill my needs because …

I do not want others to take care of me because …

Managing My Transition Experiences

Connected or Not?

Intimacy illustrates your ability to feel truly connected to other people.
For a variety of reasons, you may be feeling disconnected to important people in your life.

Complete the tables below to explore the level of your relationships with others.

People I FEEL Connected To and the Level of this Relationship	Our Relationship	Why I FEEL Connected
EXAMPLE: Sam, we've always been close.	My brother	I was able to confide in him about my trauma and he constantly checks in with me.

People I DO NOT FEEL Connected To and the Level of this Relationship	Our Relationship	Why I DO NOT Feel Connected and Do I want to Improve It?
EXAMPLE: Jane. We haven't gotten along since the trauma.	My sister	She feels I am being "overly dramatic" about the trauma and tells me to "get over it." Perhaps when I am stronger and not so affected by my trauma. Not now.

Which table was easier to complete, and why? _____

Managing Trauma Workbook

Trust

For a variety of reasons, you may be having a hard time trusting other people
Being able to trust another person means feeling safe and secure in your relationship with this person. Who are you able to trust, and who can you not trust?

Complete the table that follows to explore those people YOU TRUST.

People I TRUST	Why I Trust This Person	Have you Talked to This Person about Your Traumatic Event? Why or Why Not?
EXAMPLE: My Mom	She's always been there for me.	Yes, and she's been accepting and non-judgmental.

Complete the table that follows to explore those people you CANNOT TRUST.

People I DO NOT TRUST	Why I Do Not Trust Them	How this Affects My Ability to Deal with the Traumatic event
EXAMPLE: My Uncle	We used to be so close but recently he told other relatives that I'm to blame.	I don't have another male to talk with but he doesn't understand me or my situation.

Which table was easier to complete. Why? _____

Managing My Transition Experiences

My View of Others

Many people feel differently about people in their lives after having experienced a trauma. How do you view important others in your life?

You can use words to describe these people or draw what you think they look like.

Which people would you like to talk to about what happened to you?
Why haven't you discussed the event with these people?

_____

_____

_____

Managing Trauma Workbook

Physical Boundaries

If you have experienced a trauma in your life you possibly have, or will set up, physical boundaries that you keep with various people in your life. A physical boundary is the amount of space you feel that you need around you when interacting with other people.

Answer the following questions to explore your physical boundaries.

The amount of space I need between me and other people to feel comfortable and safe is
_____

Is this boundary the same for all people? If not, who is it different for and why?
_____
_____
_____

How do you maintain your physical boundary?
_____
_____
_____

How do you feel when someone invades your space?
_____
_____
_____

How do you react when this happens?
_____
_____
_____

How do you tell others if you feel like they are invading your space?
_____
_____

Managing My Transition Experiences

My Safety Plan

Everybody has the right to feel safe in their daily lives. Safety is the feeling of freedom from harm inflicted by you or other people. Whether you feel the need to talk to someone, or go to a safe place, there are people who can help ensure that you are safe.

In the spaces that follow, identify those people who can help you and how they can help you. In the third column, list the best method to reach each person.

People Who Can Help	How This Person Can Help	How I Can Contact This Person
EXAMPLE: My Neighbor Sally	She is a great listener	I can send her a text message.

TIPS FOR STAYING SAFE

Which do you do? Place an X in the boxes of the items you are already doing. Add your own.

- ☐ Check the locks on the doors and windows of your home.
- ☐ Take a self-defense class.
- ☐ Have an escape plan if you need one.
- ☐ Be aware of your environment.
- ☐ Avoid risky places.
- ☐ _____
- ☐ _____
- ☐ _____

Managing Trauma Workbook

Physical Safety

You need to feel physically safe and protected from harm if you are going to be able to move past the trauma you experienced. As you stay physically safe, you will remain in the present and feel grounded to make positive life decisions.

Think about the places where you either feel safe or do not feel safe.

Places	Why I Feel Safe or Not Safe in this Place	How I Can Feel Safe or More Safe in this Place
Home		
Work		
Community		
School		
Place of Worship		
Other		
Other		

Managing My Transition Experiences

Environmental Safety

You have the right to live your life free from harm from other people.

Following are some of the ways that you can develop greater environmental safety:

Remove yourself from people who are harming you or who might harm you.
How can you do this?

_____

_____

_____

_____

Know from whom you can get help and how they can help you.
Who are these people and how can they help you?

_____

_____

_____

_____

Develop an emergency escape plan. How can you do this?

_____

_____

_____

_____

Ensure you are living in a safe place. How can you do this?

_____

_____

_____

_____

Managing Trauma Workbook

Emotional Safety

People who are moving on from a traumatic event do not isolate themselves from other people. They are interested in reconnecting with people in their lives, and making new friends.

Who are the people from whom you have isolated yourself, and what can be done to fix your relationships with these people?

People I Feel Isolated From	Why I Feel This Way	What I Can do to Re-establish This
EXAMPLE: My partner	He does not understand how I feel	I can try to talk openly with him and help him to better understand what happened to me

Which relationship do you want to re-establish the most? Why?

_____

_____

_____

Managing My Transition Experiences

A Safety Contract

By filling in the blanks on this contract, you will agree to live the rest of your life safely and in a way that will not induce self-harm.

Complete the following contract and sign and date it. Keep it handy so that you can see it daily.

I, _____, agree not to harm myself in any way.
                       NAME

I will not try to escape the pain of my trauma by doing any of the following:

- Use any illegal substances such as _____
  _____
  _____

- Mutilate my body by _____
  _____
  _____

- Harm others by _____
  _____
  _____

- Engage in high-risk activities such as _____
  _____
  _____

I agree to seek professional help if I _____
_____
_____
_____
_____

_____   _____
NAME   DATE

Managing Trauma Workbook

My Safe Places

One thing you can do to feel safe is to identify or create safe places.
In thinking of your safe place, it should be where you and nobody else can access.
In this place you feel safe and secure.

In the spaces that follow, write about or draw four of your favorite safe places, and describe what allows you to feel safe in each of them.

Safe Place 1	Safe Place 2

Safe Place 3	Safe Place 4

Which of these four is the safe place that you treasure the most, and why?

Managing My Transition Experiences

Victim Thinking

Victim thinking is a fearful, negative view of life, self and the world as a result of living through a traumatic event. The following checklist will allow you to explore how much you use victim thinking.

For each of the items that follow, place a check mark in the boxes that apply to you and then write why you think these statements are true.

- ☐ I can never be loved again
- ☐ I have no control over the bad things that are going to happen
- ☐ I am afraid of the future
- ☐ Things will never get better for me
- ☐ I must be extra good to compete with other people
- ☐ I will always feel traumatized
- ☐ I will never be as good as other people
- ☐ I can never succeed
- ☐ I feel different from other people
- ☐ I cannot make my life any better than it is
- ☐ I feel like I need to apologize a lot
- ☐ I am unworthy
- ☐ I am afraid my traumatic event might happen again
- ☐ I feel misunderstood
- ☐ I am negative most of the time
- ☐ I wish the event had not happened to me

Affirmations

Following are some of the affirmations you can say to yourself to feel less like a victim.
Cut them out and put them in places where you can see them. (wallet, mirror, computer)

I am worthy just as I am!	I am lovable!	I am better every day!
I can overcome!	I can reach out when I need to!	My life matters!
I am cared about!	I am special!	I will put this behind me!

Managing Trauma Workbook

A Historical Perspective

Identify a historical figure from history whom you have always admired.
This person could be a politician, artist, writer, military officer, activist, or any other figure you admire.

Name your historical figure, explain why you admire this person, and then answer the following questions from this historical figure's perspective.

Who is the historical figure you admire?

Why do you admire this person?

If that person were alive, what would he or she say to you about the trauma you have been through?

What advice would this person have for you?

What would this person say about how you have handled the trauma you experienced?

How would this person suggest that you move on from the trauma?

From what you just wrote, how can you integrate these insights into your life?

Managing My Transition Experiences

My Angry Moments

All people become angry, but people who function well understand the situations in which they get angry, and then are able to effectively control their angry feelings.

What are some of the situations in which you express your anger inappropriately?

My Angry Moment Situation	Why I Become Angry	How I Expressed My Anger	How I Could Have Expressed it More Appropriately
Example: I get angry when people ask me to help them at work when I'm thinking about my traumatic event.	I say to myself, I'm the one who experienced a traumatic event, not them!	I am abrupt with them.	I could explain to them that I cannot take on too many tasks at this point in my life.

Which moments are negatively affecting your life the most? _____

_____

_____

_____

Managing Trauma Workbook

Constructive Vs. Destructive Anger Management

Think about some of the ways that you express anger in your life.
Some of these ways are constructive and some are probably destructive and hurt people in your life.

Whether at home, at work, in school, or in the community, describe some of the ways you express anger constructively (talking to a support person, journaling your feelings, etc.), and some of the ways you express anger destructively (destroy things, abuse others physically, emotionally, verbally, sexually, etc.).

Constructive	Destructive

Compare the items in both columns and think about whether you need to work on your anger management issues.

Managing My Transition Experiences

Why am I So Angry?

Unresolved anger is often felt by a person who has experienced a traumatic event.
This anger is intensified when reminded of the event.
It is important to explore why you feel angry about your traumatic event.

These questions will guide you through this process. Think about why you feel angry at times.

Are you angry because the trauma occurred at all? Explain.

Are you angry because the trauma happened to you? Explain.

Are you angry because you did not do more? Explain.

Are you angry because someone else suffered? Explain.

Are you angry because you have not recovered? Explain.

Are you angry because you feel like you cannot heal? Explain.

Are you angry because life just isn't fair? Explain.

Managing Trauma Workbook

Hopefulness

People who enjoy a low-level of stress and a feeling of general well-being have hopes and dreams for the future.

Explore your hopes for the future in the spaces that follow.

I hope I can …

I hope my family will …

I hope my friends will …

I hope at work I can …

I hope I don't …

I hope the people involved in my trauma …

> *Hope is being able to see that there is light despite all of the darkness.*
> *~ Desmond Tutu*

What is your light despite all of the darkness?

_____

_____

Managing My Transition Experiences

Self-Esteem

The experience of a traumatic event can cause people to question their sense of who they are. The negative effects of a trauma can be overcome by your ability to develop a positive sense of who you are as a person.

In each of the blocks that follow, write words that describe your most positive qualities.
(Example: artistic, smart, caring, love for children, etc.)

My Personality Strengths

My Talents

My Knowledge

My Special Gifts

My Strengths and Talents

Many people who have been through a traumatic event lose track of their strengths, talents, and great personality traits. Many of these losses are due to the experience they endured, but some are not.

In the spaces that follow, identify your strengths and talents.

My Strengths	**My Talents**	**My Positive Personality Traits**
(EX: perseverance)	*(drawing and painting)*	*(I am conscientious at work)*
_____	_____	_____
_____	_____	_____
_____	_____	_____
_____	_____	_____
_____	_____	_____

How did the traumatic event make you stronger? _____

_____

_____

_____

How did the traumatic event help you discover that you have more talents? _____

_____

_____

_____

How did the traumatic event strengthen you to be more able to deal with life in general? _____

_____

_____

_____

Managing My Transition Experiences

Re-Writing Your Narrative

In the spaces that follow, you have an opportunity to re-write the narrative of the traumatic event you experienced. For this activity, describe the event, but this time describe yourself as the hero/heroine of the story.

Would this have been feasible? _____

What did you learn? _____

Solving my Problem

To recover, people need to be able to solve problems well.
Worrying about your problems will not only fail to solve them, but it will also create additional stress. It is important to develop a system for solving the small or large problems you encounter in life.

Identify a problem you have encountered in life. _____
_____
_____

What are the elements of the problem? Who is involved? What happened?
_____
_____
_____

What are some possible solutions to your problem? Don't evaluate, just write them down.

_____ _____
_____ _____
_____ _____

What are the pros and cons of each of these solutions?

- What is required to implement the solution?
- Do I have the time, money and skills to carry the solution out?
- Can the solution be implemented?
- Would the people involved be cooperative?

After you have answered the precious questions for each solution, put a "Yes" or "No" next to each solution above.

Which solution provides you with the best chance of success? Why this solution?
_____
_____
_____
_____

My Life Purpose

Having a specific purpose in life can help you move on from your traumatic event. Purpose is that thing that makes you feel fulfilled in life.

In each of the spaces that follow, describe various aspect of your life purpose. If the sentence starter does not apply to you, explain why not.

My life purpose is …

_____
_____
_____

My job contributes to my life purpose in the following ways:

_____
_____
_____

My family contributes to my life purpose in the following ways:

_____
_____
_____

My interests contribute to my life purpose in the following ways:

_____
_____
_____

My education contributes to my life purpose in the following ways:

_____
_____
_____

Add Life Structure

To avoid as many triggers as possible, it is important to add structure to your life as much as possible, and to eliminate chance and chaos as much as possible.

In each of the areas, how can you structure your life to have fewer triggers?

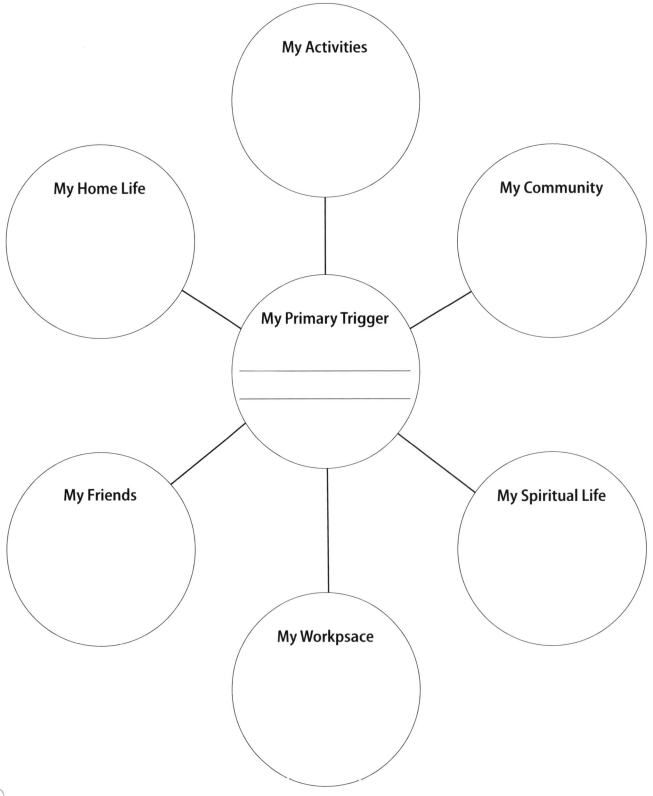

MODULE IV

Tools for Coping with My Symptoms

The memory, experiencing and re-experiencing, has such power over one's mere personal life …

~ Rebecca West

Name _____

Date _____

Managing Trauma Workbook

Module IV – Tools for Coping with My Symptoms
Skills Emphasized in Each Activity Handout

Intrusive Thoughts .... page 86
Identify eight or more intrusive thoughts one may experience, rate their frequency, and reframe each. Describe which thoughts interfere most with one's daily activities.

My Trauma Triggers .... page 87
Identify one's triggers from among twenty possibilities.

Trigger Management .... page 88
Select six or more coping mechanisms which were tried, liked, disliked and why. State reasons why one has not tried specific coping mechanisms.

My Nightmare and My Trauma .... page 89
Describe one's most frequent nightmare, its sensory experiences, its ending and how one wants it to end.

The Value of Positive Distractions .... page 90
State five unwanted thoughts, ways to distract oneself and the benefits of positive distractions.

Flashbacks .... page 91
Describe one's flashback – its timing, triggers, the persons involved and ways to cope.

My Sleep Patterns .... page 92
Quantify the extent of one's sleep problems by responding to fifteen prompts and interpreting the score.

Tracking My Sleep Patterns .... page 93
Document one's quantity and quality of sleep each day of the week. State how each day's bedtime routines and trauma-related events affected one's sleep.

Sleep Tips .... page 94
Select from among forty suggestions those that have been effective and those one is willing to try.

Jittery, Anxious? Edgy? Jumpy? Agitated? Worried? Scared? Skittish? ...... page 95
Identify six factors that worsen one's anxiety, one's previous reactions and ways to gain perspective.

Over-Cautious? .... page 96
Select six or more examples that suggest one is over-cautious. State reasons and ways to cope.

Problem Solving for the Overly-Cautious .... page 97
Complete five sentences to personalize one's overly-cautious behavior. State how each reaction presents a problem and ways to cope.

Anticipating High-Risk Situations .... page 98
Describe five high-risk situations, when they are encountered, one's reactions and ways to cope.

COPING: Let's Meditate .... page 99
Practice three meditation steps and state one's reaction. Use the meditation technique again in response to a stressful thought and evaluate its effectiveness.

COPING: Deep Breathing .... page 100
Read a quotation, plus five ways that illustrate the benefits of deep breathing. Practice three steps, then plan ways to use the technique and to overcome anticipated obstacles.

COPING: Mindfulness and Paying Attention .... page 101
Practice four mindfulness steps. Journal about any difficulties with the process and share the beneficial effects on one's thoughts and feelings.

COPING: Total-Body Relaxation .... page 102
Practice seventeen Total Body Relaxation (Progressive Muscle Relaxation) steps.

Ways to Make Meaning .... page 103
Identify ways one was helped by the trauma by completing nine sentence starters.

Tools for Coping with My Symptoms Scale
Introduction and Directions

Healing from a trauma is often accomplished when the trauma is processed and accepted as a part of your life experience. Many people want to escape from their painful memories, only to find that memories are triggered by many ordinary life occurrences and will continue to reoccur. By being aware of this, one can learn to manage symptoms.

This scale contains 30 statements related to how you re-experience the memories of the trauma in your life. Read each of the statements and decide how much the statement describes you.

- If the statement describes you a lot, circle the number under that column next to that item.
- If the statement describes you sometimes, circle the number under that column next to that item.
- If the statement describes you only a little or not at all, circle the number under that column next to that item.

In the following example, the circled number under "A Lot" indicates the statement is descriptive of the person completing the inventory a lot of the time.

WHEN I BEGIN TO RE-EXPERIENCE MY TRAUMA....	A LOT	SOMETIMES	LITTLE/NONE
I am not able to remember details of the event	3	2	1

This is not a test. Since there are no right or wrong answers, do not spend too much time thinking about your answers. Be sure to respond to every statement.

(Turn to the next page and begin.)

Managing Trauma Workbook

Tools for Coping with My Symptoms Scale

WHEN I BEGIN TO RE-EXPERIENCE MY TRAUMA….	A LOT	SOMETIMES	LITTLE/NONE
I am not able to remember details of the event	3	2	1
I am jumpy and jittery	3	2	1
I am overprotective of those I love	3	2	1
I am so fearful I can't concentrate	3	2	1
I am unusually cautious	3	2	1
I become lightheaded or dizzy	3	2	1
I can hardly breathe or I breathe rapidly	3	2	1
I cannot cope with the memories	3	2	1
I can't feel calm, even in safe places	3	2	1
I experience unwanted memories of the traumatic event	3	2	1
I fear my scary nightmares and don't know what they mean	3	2	1
I feel like the trauma is happening to me right now	3	2	1
I feel my blood pressure rising	3	2	1
I feel my chest tightening	3	2	1
I feel my heart beating faster	3	2	1
I feel on guard at all times	3	2	1
I feel tingling in my hands or have sweaty palms	3	2	1
I find that unexpected things trigger my memories of the event	3	2	1
I have flashbacks of the event	3	2	1
I have hallucination-like nightmares about the event	3	2	1
I have stomach issues	3	2	1
I try to go to sleep but keep remembering	3	2	1
I look for exits in stores, movies and restaurants	3	2	1
I scan over my shoulder a lot	3	2	1
I scare easily	3	2	1
I sense reliving the moment of the event	3	2	1
I start crying when I remember	3	2	1
I suffer from pains in different parts of my body	3	2	1
I sweat profusely	3	2	1
I want to have a weapon with me at all times	3	2	1

Total = _____

Go to the Scoring Directions

Tools for Coping with My Symptoms Scale Scoring Directions

Your ability to move past the trauma that you have experienced largely depends on your ability to recall your memories in enough detail to explore what really happened and integrate the experience into your other memories. This scale is designed to help you understand and identify the symptoms when you begin to re-experience symptoms of your trauma.

Add the numbers that you circled. Your total will range from 30 to 90. Then, transfer this total to the space below:

Re-Experiencing Symptoms Total   = _____

Profile Interpretation

Individual Score	Result	Indications
0 - 49	Low	Low scores indicate that you are experiencing a low level of symptoms.
50 - 70	Moderate	Moderate scores indicate that you are experiencing a medium level of symptoms.
71 - 90	High	High scores indicate that you are experiencing a high level of symptoms.

Tools for Coping with My Symptoms Scale Description

People scoring High on this scale may be re-experiencing their trauma through symptoms related to their body; re-experiencing them through memories and flashbacks; and re-experiencing them through their intuition. Some people experience the opposite – emotional numbness and/or they mentally block out the event. They are constantly reminded of their traumatic event.

Managing Trauma Workbook

Intrusive Thoughts

Following are some of the most intrusive thoughts that people who have experienced trauma tend to have. Which ones do you experience? Complete the table that follows. If these thoughts do not occur to you, just write N/A (Does Not Apply).

My Thoughts	How Often I Have These Thoughts	How I Can Reframe These Thought
Example: I am a victim.	Every time the least little negative thing happens to me, I blame the trauma.	Little, stressful everyday stressors happen to everyone, regardless of whether they experienced a trauma or not!
I am a victim.		
My troubles are the fault of others.		
I can't trust people anymore.		
Other people blame me.		
I'll never feel safe again.		
It will happen again.		
I handled the trauma badly.		
I'm a coward.		
Other		

Which of the thoughts interfere on your life enough to interfere with you daily activities? _____
_____
_____

How can you overcome these types of thoughts? _____
_____

Tools for Coping with My Symptoms

My Trauma Triggers

It is important to explore the triggers of stressful reactions after you have experienced a trauma.

**The following will help you examine what reminds you of your trauma.
Place an X in the boxes that apply to you.
Then, in the space after each item you check, describe how the item applies to you.
The area with the most boxes checked is your greatest source of triggers.**

☐ When I see _____
☐ When I hear _____
☐ When I smell _____
☐ When I taste _____
☐ When I feel _____

Senses TOTAL = _____

☐ When I move a certain way _____
☐ When my body is in a certain position _____
☐ When I am touched a certain way _____
☐ When I feel internal sensations (headache, heartbeat) _____
☐ When I feel tension _____

Physical TOTAL = _____

☐ When I see or hear about a sad situation _____
☐ When certain seasons come along _____
☐ When I feel threatened in any way _____
☐ When important dates are upcoming _____
☐ When a certain time of day approaches _____

Emotional TOTAL = _____

☐ When I feel really stressed _____
☐ When I am in a situation similar to the situation in which
   the trauma occurred _____
☐ When I argue with others _____
☐ When I experience a major change in my life _____
☐ When I experience upheaval in my life _____

Stressful Events TOTAL = _____

Managing Trauma Workbook

Trigger Management

Rather than giving into the distress caused by intrusive thoughts, it is better to try and manage the stress.

Think back over the past week, and describe which types of coping mechanisms you used, how effective they were, and the end result.
Complete this table to identify effective trigger-management techniques.

Techniques	Tried and Liked it. Why I Like it.	Have Not Tried it. Why I Haven't.	Tried it and Do Not Like it. Why I Don't.
EXAMPLE: Breathing	When I feel a trigger to my trauma, I try to find a quiet place, close my eyes and focus on my breathing. I take deep breaths and count them.		
Relaxation – Find a quiet place to relax, meditate, yoga, soothing music, guided imagery, draw, write, etc.			
Breathing – Take some time to simply breathe. Take deep breaths in through your nose and breathe out through your mouth.			
Prescribed Medications – Be sure that you have taken your medications that were prescribed by a physician.			
Visualization – Think about your safe place and visualize that you are there and feel totally relaxed and safe.			
Social Support – Confide in and talk with trusted friends and family about your stress and anxiety.			
Distract Myself – Find ways to take your mind off your anxiety.			
Other			
Other			

Tools for Coping with My Symptoms

My Nightmare and My Trauma

Many people who experience trauma have recurring nightmares that interfere with their sleep.

Explore the effects of your nightmare.

Do you know what triggers your nightmare? _____

What is it? _____

_____

_____

_____

_____

_____

How does your nightmare affect you afterwards? _____

_____

_____

_____

_____

_____

How does your nightmare interfere with your next day's activities? _____

_____

_____

_____

_____

_____

It helps to understand nightmares. Who is a trusting person with whom you can talk to about your nightmares? _____

_____

_____

_____

The Value of Positive Distractions

Distraction from unwanted thoughts may help take your mind off your trauma for a while.

What are some of the ways you can distract yourself in a positive way?

My Unwanted Thoughts	How I Can Distract Myself	How This Can Helps Me
Example: I am reminded of my trauma.	I can read a good book or listen to an audio book.	I get absorbed in the book and only think about the story not my trauma.

Flashbacks

Flashbacks occur when you feel as if a trauma from the past takes you back, and is occurring to you in the here and now.

Think back to the last time you experienced a flashback and answer the questions that follow.

When a flashback occurs, when does it usually happen?

___

Who is involved when it usually occurs?

___

What do you think triggered it?

___

What can you do the next time it happens?

___

My Sleep Patterns

You might have trouble falling asleep and staying asleep. By exploring your sleep patterns, you can discover some of the reasons you are not getting adequate amounts of sleep.

For the assessment that follows, rate your sleep patterns by circling the appropriate number.

1 = If it happens very seldom or not at all
2 = If it happens some of the time
3 = If it happens most of the time

I have trouble falling asleep at night	3	2	1
I awaken too early in the morning	3	2	1
I make mistakes during the day because I'm tired	3	2	1
I have scary nightmares	3	2	1
I am restless while sleeping	3	2	1
I wake up in a few hours and then can't go back to sleep	3	2	1
I dream weird dreams	3	2	1
I am sleepy during the day	3	2	1
I feel tired when I wake up	3	2	1
I have body movements with my bad dreams	3	2	1
I have nightmares early and then I am too upset to sleep	3	2	1
I can't fall asleep because I have unwanted thoughts	3	2	1
I rarely get a good night's sleep	3	2	1
I get up to go to the bathroom and then think unhappy thoughts	3	2	1
I dream about an exact replay of my trauma in another situation	3	2	1

**Now count the total of the numbers you circled above.
If your total score was between 15 and 25, you probably are having some sleep problems.
If your total score was between 26 and 35, you are probably having many sleep problems.
If your total score was between 36 and 45, you are probably having major sleep problems.**

Tools for Coping with My Symptoms

Tracking My Sleep Patterns

If you are experiencing sleep problems, it may be helpful for you to keep track of exactly how much sleep you get each night. A sleep journal can help you to identify the days when you do not get adequate or restful sleep, and the possible reasons.

Complete the following sleep diary information each night.

Day of the Week	Total Hours of Sleep	My Bedtime Routine	Quality of Sleep 1 = not good 5 = great	What happened this day related to my trauma
Monday				
Tuesday				
Wednesday				
Thursday				
Friday				
Saturday				
Sunday				

What is the relationship between your bedtime routine and what happens during the day and your sleep? _____

_____

Managing Trauma Workbook

Sleep Tips

If you are not getting restorative or adequate sleep at night, you need to work to improve your chances of good sleep. The good news is that you can do a many things to improve your chances of getting better sleep. Some of the techniques you can try to get better sleep at night are listed below.

Put a check (✓) in the boxes of the items that have been effective for you.

Put a plus (+) in the boxes of the items that you are willing to try.

- ☐ Avoid drinking too many liquids in the evening
- ☐ Be sure your bed is comfortable
- ☐ Block out noises with earplugs
- ☐ Decide to have no rich foods within two hours of bedtime
- ☐ Do not eat spicy foods in the evening
- ☐ Don't watch television
- ☐ Eat a light snack if you are hungry at bedtime
- ☐ Eliminate loud noises
- ☐ Engage in something mildly stimulating after dinner to avoid falling asleep too early
- ☐ Enjoy a warm bath or shower before bed
- ☐ Exercise regularly 20-30 minutes in the morning or early afternoon, not at night
- ☐ Go to sleep at the same time each day
- ☐ Have the same sleep routine on weekends
- ☐ If taking a nap, do it in the early afternoon
- ☐ Journal
- ☐ Keep televisions or computers out of the bedroom
- ☐ Listen to a book on tape
- ☐ Maintain a bedtime routine
- ☐ Make sure the room temperature is set comfortably
- ☐ Meditate
- ☐ Mentally, repeat soothing words
- ☐ Only use the bedroom for sleep and sex
- ☐ Prepare before bedtime for the next day
- ☐ Promote only a soft light in the bedroom
- ☐ Read a book or magazine
- ☐ Relax with progressive relaxation exercise
- ☐ Resist caffeine after noon time
- ☐ Rest to relaxing music
- ☐ Say no to alcohol and nicotine before bedtime
- ☐ Set the temperature or open windows for a cool room
- ☐ Stay away from big meals close to bedtime
- ☐ Stretches easily before bed
- ☐ Take medications as prescribed
- ☐ Try deep breathing exercise
- ☐ Use guided imagery
- ☐ Wake up at the same time each day
- ☐ When you wake up and can't go back to sleep in 15 minutes, do a non-stimulating activity
- ☐ Wind down the evening with a favorite hobby
- ☐ Write ideas and plans on paper next to the bed and then fall asleep

Tools for Coping with My Symptoms

Jittery? Anxious? Edgy? Jumpy? Agitated? Worried? Scared? Skittish?

Often when people are overly cautious because of their trauma, they become more jittery, anxious, edgy, jumpy, agitated, worried, scared and/or skittish than usual.

Which of the words above describe you? _____

Below, write the types of noises, actions, or events make you more so than usual, what happens and what can you do about it?

This makes me more _____ *word(s) you wrote on the line above*	When this happens, I …	To put this situation in perspective I can …

Managing Trauma Workbook

Over Cautious?

Often people who have experienced a traumatic event become over cautious. However, this can be taken to an extreme and cause more anxiety and fear than necessary.

Explore ways you may be over-cautious.

Ways I am Over-Cautious	Why I Feel Like This	How I can Avoid being Over-Cautious
EXAMPLE: I feel like I'm on guard all of the time.	I am scared that the trauma situation will happen again!	Replace my over-the-top negative thoughts with reality-based thoughts.
I feel like I'm on guard all of the time.		
I am too cautious.		
I always look over my shoulder.		
I am overprotective.		
I don't feel safe.		
I startle easily.		
I don't trust others.		
I am ready to flee.		
Other		

Which of your over-cautious behaviors concern you the most? What will you do about it?

_____

_____

Tools for Coping with My Symptoms

Problem Solving for the Overly-Cautious

Constantly scanning the environment for signs of danger can be a problematic for survivors.

In the spaces that follow, write about how acting overly-cautious makes your life stressful.

Overly Cautious	Why This Presents a Problem To Me in My Life	What I Can Do About It
EXAMPLE: I am in a perpetual state of fear when *I take an airplane*	I can't visit my sister in another country.	I can learn to use coping methods such as mediation or deep breathing.
I am in a perpetual state of fear when _____		
I don't feel prepared to cope with _____		
I am worried I will be too preoccupied about _____		
I am unable to connect with others because _____		
I am missing out on _____ when others in my life _____		
Other _____		

Managing Trauma Workbook

Anticipating High-Risk Situations

There are avoidable triggers of your trauma. It is important to be aware of and to identify your high-risk situations, and be prepared to deal with the stress that will arise.

What are your high-risk situations and how can you cope with them more effectively?

My High-Risk Situations	When I Encounter this Situation	How I React	How I Can Cope
EXAMPLE: Walk in the park at night.	I take my dog for a walk after I get home from work.	I get sweaty, begin to feel dizzy, and have trouble breathing.	Find a safe place to walk.

What high-risk situation is particularly worrisome? _____

_____

What steps could you immediately take to feel less stressed in that situation? _____

_____

_____

Tools for Coping with My Symptoms

COPING: Let's Meditate

There are many misconceptions about what meditation is and how to meditate. Meditation is easy and helps you relax, become calm and stop the thoughts about the event from flooding back into your consciousness.

Here is the process:

1. Right now, think of something that is calming to you, such as sitting on a beach, a vase full of flowers, your favorite pet, walking in the woods, or the face of someone you love.

2. With this image in your mind, gently close your eyes and focus on this image.

3. After a few seconds, open your eyes.

How did it feel?

_____
_____
_____
_____

What thoughts popped back into your head?

_____
_____
_____
_____

4. Now try again and this time as the thoughts pop into your head, let them dissolve and refocus your attention on the image.

How did it feel now?

_____
_____
_____
_____

Keep practicing this daily for five to ten minutes, and you will notice your anxiety becoming less prominent.

COPING: Deep Breathing

> *When you own your breath, nobody can steal your peace.*
> *~ Author Unknown*

Deep breathing can help you in a variety of ways:

- Reduces hyperventilation when you encounter a trigger
- Helps you feel more at peace
- Helps you sleep better
- Reduces everyday stress
- Reduces panic and anxiety

1. Scan your body and identify the parts that are the most tense and list them.

   _____
   _____

2. Next, inhale slowly through your nose until you see your abdomen rising. Hold this breath for five seconds.

3. Then, exhale through your mouth slowly, pushing all of the air out. Do this again five times until you feel more relaxed.

How can you use this technique when a trigger causes you to remember the trauma?

_____
_____
_____

What obstacles do you anticipate in using this technique?

_____
_____
_____

How can you overcome these obstacles?

_____
_____

COPING: Mindfulness and Paying Attention

Mindfulness is the skill of attending fully to any experience you encounter. Being mindful can lessen the impact and help you to step back from thoughts and feelings about your trauma without reacting.

Let's practice mindfulness now.
1. Look around you and focus on something of interest to you.
2. Concentrate on the object.
3. Each time your mind begins to wander from the object, bring it back to full attention.
4. Do this for several minutes.
5. Then journal about the following questions.

How did you feel during the activity?

_____
_____
_____
_____

Did you have difficulty attending to the object? If so, why?

_____
_____
_____
_____

What did you notice about your thoughts as you mindfully attended to the object?

_____
_____
_____
_____

How can this help you?

_____
_____
_____
_____

Managing Trauma Workbook

COPING: Total-Body Relaxation

Anxiety manifests itself through physical symptoms in your body.
These physical symptoms often reinforce your anxiety-producing thoughts and feelings.
Total-Body Relaxation (often called Progressive Muscle Relaxation) is a simple technique used to stop anxiety by relaxing all of the muscles throughout your body one group at a time.

Read through the following script several times before you attempt to do this exercise.

1. *Take a few deep breaths, and begin to relax.*
2. *Get comfortable and put aside all of your worries.*
3. *Let each part of your body begin to relax ... starting with your feet.*
4. *Imagine your feet relaxing as all of your tension begins to fade away.*
5. *Imagine the relaxation moving up into your calves and thighs ...feel them beginning to relax.*
6. *Continue now to let the relaxation move into your hips.*
7. *Allow the relaxation to move into your waist and stomach.*
8. *Your entire body from the waist down is now completely relaxed.*
9. *Let go of any strain and discomfort you might feel.*
10. *Allow the relaxation to move into your chest until your chest feels completely relaxed.*
11. *Just enjoy the feeling of complete relaxation.*
12. *Continue to let the relaxation move through the muscles of your shoulders, then spread down into your upper arms, into your elbows, and finally all the way down to your wrists and hands.*
13. *Put aside all of your worries.*
14. *Let yourself be totally present in the moment and let yourself relax more and more. Let all the muscles in your neck unwind and let the relaxation move into your chin and jaws.*
15. *Feel the tension around your eyes flow away as the relaxation moves throughout your face and head.*
16. *Feel your forehead relax and your entire head beginning to feel lighter.*
17. *Let yourself drift deeper and deeper into relaxation and peace.*

After you have read the above paragraph several times, find a quiet location where you can practice Total-Body Relaxation.

Assume a comfortable position in a chair.

Take off your jewelry and glasses so that you are totally free.

Try to let the relaxation happen without having to force it.

If during the relaxation you lose concentration, don't be concerned - just begin again.

Tools for Coping with My Symptoms

Ways to Make Meaning

As a result of the trauma you have experienced, you are changed. An important aspect in healing is to make sense of the trauma that happened to you.

Think about ways that the trauma has HELPED you, and answer the following sentence starters that apply to you. If any do not apply to you, explain in that space.

I can tolerate anything else that happens to me including _____
_____
_____

I can see a cause that I could champion such as _____
_____
_____

I will take care of myself for the rest of my life by _____
_____
_____

I have changed for the better in the following ways: _____
_____
_____

I accept that what happened to me was not my fault and _____
_____
_____

I have greater will power that shows up when I _____
_____
_____

I am more persistent as evidenced by _____
_____
_____

I am closer to the following people: _____
_____
_____

I feel like my purpose in life is to _____
_____
_____

MODULE V

Erasing the Stigma of Mental Health Issues

Stigma's power lies in silence. The silence that persists when discussion and action should be taking place …

~ *M.B. Dallocchio*

Name _____

Date _____

Module V – Erasing the Stigma of Mental Health Issues
Skills Emphasized in Each Activity Handout

Two Types of Mental Health Stigma . . . . page 108
  Describe types of stigma and prejudice endured due to trauma.

The Stigma of Trauma – THE PAST . . . . page 109
  Share feelings about past disclosures.

The Stigma of Trauma – THE PRESENT . . . . page 110
  Identify gains and losses, whom to tell, and how.

Speak Your Mind . . . . page 111
  Personalize a quotation about independent thinking by responding to five questions.

If We Stamp Out the Stigma … . . . . page 112
  Journal about a quote to help shed shame and fear.

Glenn Close said … . . . . page 113
  State ways talking about issues promotes healing.

Effects of Trauma Issues . . . . page 114
  Name eight persons who may help in stigma-related situations.

The Stigma of Going to a Mental Health Therapist . . . . page 115
  Discuss concerns; commit to seeing a counselor if needed.

Stereotypes . . . . page 116
  Document ways one refutes six stereotypes.

Will You Speak Out? . . . . page 117
  Describe ways individuals and the group can help erase stigma.

My Negative Thoughts . . . . page 118
  Identify six negative assumptions; use a physical thought-stopping technique.

Focus on Your Strengths . . . . page 119
  State ways to demonstrate strengths in five areas of life.

Ways I Try to Minimize My Trauma Stress . . . . page 120
  Respond to six examples: tell effects on self, others, and better ways to cope.

Ways I am Treated . . . . page 121
  Describe eight ways one is treated, plus self-treatment.

Self-Doubt . . . . page 122
  Describe five ways to stop the self-defeating process.

A Poster about the STIGMA of People Who Have Experienced a Trauma . . . . page 123
  Show perceptions of being stigmatized due to trauma.

A Poster about ACCEPTANCE of People Who Have Experienced a Trauma . . . . page 124
  Show how reaction to trauma looks when one is accepted.

DE-STIGMA-TIZE with the Facts about Mental Health Issues . . . . page 125
  Acknowledge eight myths, corresponding facts, and the value of seeking help.

Coping with the Stigma of a Mental Health Issue . . . . page 126
  Personalize five suggestions; state ways to follow through.

Speak Out Against Stigmas . . . . page 127
  State five ways to advocate and the benefits to self and others.

Erasing the Stigma of Mental Health Issues
Introduction

A stigma is extreme social disapproval of some type of personal characteristic or a belief that is not considered socially "acceptable." People who have a particular attribute considered unwanted by society are rejected or stigmatized as a result of the attribute. People who have experienced traumatic events in the past are often judged unfairly to be crazy, violent, unpredictable, explosive, aggressive and/or unstable. These judgments, or social stigmas, can cause people who experience these issues to feel devalued as human beings. They are often ostracized from activities, rejected in social situations, stereotyped, minimized in the workplace, and shunned by others. People experiencing the stigma of reactions to traumatic events often feel extreme physical, emotional and psychological distress.

People who stigmatize and/or stereotype others bring about unfair treatment rather than help. This unfair treatment can be very obvious. For example, people make negative comments or laugh. On the other hand, this unfair treatment can be very subtle. For example - people assume that a person who experiences trauma issues is detached, emotionless, irritable or grumpy and they avoid or shun that person.

Stigmas affect a large percentage of people throughout the world. Some of the more common stigmas are associated with physical disabilities, mental health issues, age, body type, gender, sexual orientation, nationality, religion, family, ethnicity, race, religion, financial status, social sub-cultures, and conduct. Stigmas set people apart from society and produce feelings in them of shame and isolation. People who are stigmatized are often considered socially unacceptable, and they suffer prejudice, rejection, avoidance and discrimination.

What Can Be Done?
Fear of judgment and ridicule about suffering from a traumatic experience often compels individuals and their families to hide from society rather than face criticism, shunning, labeling and stereotyping. Instead of seeking treatment, they struggle in silence. Let's discuss some ways you can combat the stereotypes and stigmas associated with these issues.

- You and your loved ones have choices. You can decide who is to know about your trauma and what to tell them. You need not feel guilty, ashamed or embarrassed.

- You are not alone. Remember that many other people are coping with a similar situation.

- Look into or start a support group to meet others who experience what you do.

- Seek help and remember that the activities in this workbook and treatment from medical professionals can help you to have a productive education and career, and live a satisfying life.

- Be proactive and surround yourself with supportive people – people you can trust. Social isolation is a negative side effect of the stigma linked to reactions to traumatic events. Isolating yourself and discontinuing enjoyable activities will not help.

How Can This Section Help Me?
Managing Trauma Workbook is designed to help you deal more effectively with your issues, and this section is specifically designed to help you overcome the stigma attached to those issues. Complete the activities that follow to help you to appreciate yourself, feel content, and become more resilient in the face of your trauma issues.

Two Types of Mental Health Stigma

Mental health stigma can be divided into two types:

1. **Social stigma** is characterized by prejudicial attitudes and discriminating behavior directed towards individuals with mental health issues.

2. **Perceived stigma** is the internalizing by the people with mental health issues of their understanding of discrimination.

What do you think are the differences between these two types of stigmas?

_____
_____
_____
_____

Describe a time when you faced prejudice or discrimination because you experienced a traumatic event.

_____
_____
_____
_____

Describe a time when you felt like you were at a disadvantage because you experienced a traumatic event.

_____
_____
_____
_____

Often one perceives others' stigmatizing, or exaggerates others' or their own reactions.

Erasing the Stigma of Mental Health Issues

The Stigma of Trauma – THE PAST

People who experience a traumatic event in their lives are prone to reoccurring symptoms. When this happens, they often have a stigma placed on them by other people. Often the stigma attached to these issue stops one from moving forward - being unable to talk about it for fear of being judged or labeled. We can erase the stigma of any mental health issues by starting to discuss it with one person at a time, and taking the time to explain the traumatic events you lived through in the past.

Let's start with people with whom you have already shared your story.

With whom have you discussed your issues?	What did you say?	What was this person's reaction? What did the person say?	How did you feel?
Family			
Friends			
Acquaintances			
People in your community or your house of worship			
Mental Health Professionals			
Other			

If any one of the above reacted in a negative way, to what do you attribute that reaction?

_____

_____

_____

The Stigma of Trauma – THE PRESENT

If you are willing to tell your story to people, now may be the time. This workbook has helped you to organize your thoughts and feelings about what happened to you. One of the ways to erase this stigma is to talk about it and let others know that people who have these issues are just like anyone else who have some type of an issue.

Perhaps it is time to talk with other people whom you trust and/or with whom you feel safe.

Person with whom you might discuss your issue?	What would you say to this person?	What do you think this person's reaction might be?	What could you gain or lose by discussing it with this person?
Family			
Friends			
Acquaintances			
People in your community or your house of worship			
Mental Health Professionals			
Other			

Brainstorm:

At what point, in a serious relationship, is it time to discuss your issues?

Speak Your Mind

> *Follow the path of the unsafe, independent thinker. Expose your ideas to the danger of controversy. Speak your mind and fear less the label of 'crackpot' than the stigma of conformity.*
> *~ Thomas J. Watson*

What does this quote mean to you? _____
_____
_____
_____

Have you spoken your mind? Why not? _____
_____
_____
_____

Are you worried about being labeled? _____
_____
_____
_____

How can you expose your ideas to others? _____
_____
_____
_____

What is keeping you from telling your story? _____
_____
_____
_____

If We Stamp Out the Stigma …

Journal your thoughts about the following quotation and describe how you can do your part to erase the stigma of trauma issues:

> *If we stamp out the stigma attached to mental health issues, shed the shame and eliminate the fear, then we open the door for people to speak freely about what they are feeling and thinking.*
> ~ *Jaletta Albright Desmond*

Erasing the Stigma of Mental Health Issues

Glenn Close said ...

"The most powerful way to change someone's view is to meet them ... People who do come out and talk about mental illness, that's when healing can really begin. You can lead a productive life."

Name a time when you have changed someone else's view – about anything. _____
_____
_____

How did that feel to you? _____
_____
_____

Name a time you were tempted to talk about your trauma issues, but didn't? Why not? _____
_____
_____

Write about a situation in which you DID talk about your trauma issues. _____
_____
_____
_____
_____

How did that feel? _____

How did it work out? _____

Who is a trusted person you can talk with and begin to heal? _____

Anyone else? _____

Who is a trusted person you can ask for a referral of someone to talk with in order to begin to heal?
_____

Anyone else? _____

In an ideal world, how can you lead a more stable life? _____
_____
_____

How can you contribute to changing stigma? _____
_____
_____

Managing Trauma Workbook

Effects of Trauma Issues

Check out these harmful effects of the stigma of traumatic events.

On the lines next to each item, explain if it has affected you in some way and how.

1. Lack of understanding by family _____
   _____

2. Lack of understanding by friends _____
   _____

3. Lack of understanding by co-workers, supervisors and/or customers _____
   _____

4. Discrimination at work _____
   _____

5. Inability to join community programs _____
   _____

6. Abuse: physical, emotional, verbal or sexual _____
   _____

7. Pressure from friends _____
   _____

8. The belief that you will never be able to succeed or that you can't improve your situation.
   _____
   _____

On the line of the corresponding number, write the name of a person you can speak to, a person who might help to support you about each of the situations you noted above. Add a reason for each person you have chosen.

1. _____
2. _____
3. _____
4. _____
5. _____
6. _____
7. _____
8. _____

Erasing the Stigma of Mental Health Issues

The Stigma of Going to a Mental Health Therapist

Many people have pre-conceived ideas about anyone seeking therapy.

Do you know of anyone who has gone to a mental health therapist? Write what you know about the experience. _____
_____
_____

Here are some facts about mental health and mental health therapy.

- Mental health includes how you act, feel and think in different situations.
- Mental health problems can be caused by many different things including medical health issues, abuse (emotional, physical, verbal, sexual), stress, worry, loss of a relationship, food issues, self-injuries, ADHD, STD's, family changes, addictions, traumatic events, problems, wanting to build up self-confidence, etc.
- If someone goes to a mental health therapist, this does NOT mean the person is crazy. Doctors and mental health therapists treat people the same as any other doctor treats problems (broken leg, diabetes, cancer, etc.).
- There needs to be a good connection between you and the therapist. Your therapist should be someone you feel you can trust.
- This might take a few meetings and/or a few therapists, to find the right one for you.
- Non-judgmental people who truly care about you will not judge you in a negative way. They will be proud of you for seeking help.
- The therapist does not assume that you have a mental illness. The therapist assumes something is troubling you, knows that no one leads a perfect life, and admires you for trying to make changes in your life.
- The therapist's job is to help you understand what's going on.
- The therapist will not tell you how to live your life, or how to think, act or believe.
- The therapist is not an advice-giver, but will help you think about how to improve your quality of life.
- The therapist may have some thoughts, and with you, will help you make changes.
- The therapist can help you to increase your life management skills.
- The therapist will help you recognize and express your feelings in a healthy way.
- The only person who can "fix" your problems is you, but a therapist will help you with an action plan.
- The mental health therapist may suggest that you see a medical doctor for medication.
- Therapy can be a slow or long process. Being open and honest, and wanting to feel better, will make the difference.

Place an X by the facts that you were not aware of.

What worries you about talking with a mental health therapist? _____
_____
_____

After learning about these facts, can you make a commitment to speak with a counselor or therapist?

signature _____

Managing Trauma Workbook

Stereotypes

The social stigmas about trauma often translate into the following inaccurate stereotypes.

In the table below, write about how you are unlike the stereotype provided.

Stereotype	How I Defy that Stereotype
They are damaged	
They show no emotions	
They have a victim mentality	
They can't do things	
They feel entitled	
They want people to feel sorry for them	
Other stereotypes of trauma stress	

What would you like to say to other people who label you with these or other stereotypical words?

_____

_____

Will You Speak Out?

> *Ten people who speak make more noise than ten thousand who are silent.*
> *~ Napoleon Bonaparte*

How can YOU speak out to erase the stigma of mental health issues?

_____
_____
_____
_____
_____
_____
_____
_____
_____
_____

Brainstorm with a few other people about how your group can speak out to erase the stigma of mental health issues.

_____
_____
_____
_____
_____
_____
_____
_____
_____
_____

Managing Trauma Workbook

My Negative Thoughts

You can begin to overcome the stigma related to trauma issues by refusing to worry about what others think. When you are worried about what others say about you, or might say about you, you will have a difficult time enjoying life.

What are the negative thoughts that go through your head about others and what they think of you?

Others think I am …

Others don't think I can …

Others probably find me …

I think others might be afraid or wary of me because …

Others label me as …

This makes me feel …

Now that you have written these thoughts, take a big heavy black marker and put a big **X** through all of the thoughts above. When these negative thoughts come into your head, picture that big X, reminding you not to worry about what others think.

Erasing the Stigma of Mental Health Issues

Focus on Your Strengths

You can do many things to help fight the stigma associated with your issue. You can focus on your strengths rather than your limitations. Demonstrate to others, and yourself, that you have a great deal to offer.

In the spaces that follow, identify some of your strengths. You have much to share, so take a few minutes to think about and write about some of your greatest strengths.

My strengths related to the community:

_____

_____

My strengths related to relationships with others:

_____

_____

My strengths related to my work or volunteer job:

_____

_____

My strengths related to creativity:

_____

_____

My strengths related to special skills I possess:

_____

_____

How can you share these strengths to show others that despite and/or because of your traumatic event issues, you are a talented human being?

_____

_____

Ways I Try to Minimize My Trauma Stress

Many people dealing with the stress that occurs after a traumatic event will try a variety of ways to minimize its stigma.

Complete the following table to explore the various ways that you minimize your issues and how this makes you feel. Describe some better ways to cope.

Ways I Minimize My Traumatic Event Issues	The Effect This Has on Me and Others	A Better way to Cope
Example: *I pretend that nothing is wrong with me.*	*Others think I should just get over it and move on with my life.*	*Explain and say that I've been having some recurring nightmares of my trauma and I'm working to cope.*
I pretend that nothing is wrong with me		
I refuse to get help		
I say things like "Nothing can ever help me"		
I will not talk about my mental health issues		
I laugh and make jokes about my actions		
I avoid people		
Other		

Erasing the Stigma of Mental Health Issues

Ways I Am Treated

Think about some of the ways that people treat you because of the symptoms you show.

In the spaces below, explore the various ways people treat you. Write about those who treat you unfairly and why.

I am rejected by family …

[   ]

I am rejected by my friends …

[   ]

I encounter problems at work …

[   ]

I encounter problems at home …

[   ]

I am subjected to physical violence or harassment …

[   ]

I am laughed at …

[   ]

I treat myself unfairly by …

[   ]

I treat myself fairly by …

[   ]

Managing Trauma Workbook

Self-Doubt

Don't let stigma create self-doubt and shame. One of the most important ways to minimize the stigma of a trauma is to explore how one doubts oneself. Self-doubt almost always stems from a lack of understanding rather than information based on the facts. Feeling ashamed, embarrassed or guilty because of what you experienced can be self-defeating.

How does the stress associated with having lived through a traumatic event cause you to doubt yourself, and how can you control your self-doubt in a positive and strong way?

Ways I Doubt Myself	How This Negatively Affects Me	What I Can Do About it

> *However you arrive at the ability to ignore self-doubt - if you can acquire it or possess it or find it or discover it – move beyond self-doubt.*
> ~ *Dwight Yoakum*

How do you relate to this quotation? _____

Erasing the Stigma of Mental Health Issues

A Poster about the STIGMA of People Who have Experienced a Trauma

In the space below, draw a collage of pictures, symbols and/or words, of how you believe you are being stigmatized by others.

A Poster about ACCEPTANCE of People who have Experienced a Trauma

In the space that follows, draw a collage of pictures, symbols and/or words, of what you believe that the stress related to a personal trauma looks like when you are accepted.

DE-STIGMA-TIZE with the Facts about Mental Health Issues

Myth: Mental health issues are rare.
   Fact: Mental health issues are not rare and affect nearly everyone either directly or indirectly.

Myth: People with mental health issues are unable to lead successful, productive lives.
   Fact: Most people with a mental health issues respond to treatment, learn to cope with and manage their problems, and go on to lead productive and fulfilling lives.

Myth: People who have mental health issues will not get better.
   Fact: Once diagnosed, mental health issues are treatable. While they are not always cured, they can be managed effectively. Most people with mental health issues live productive and positive lives. Many receive therapy and medications. Individuals with severe or persistent mental health issues who do not respond well to therapy or meds may require more support, or different therapists or meds, and they do well; and some may not function as highly as others.

Myth: People with mental health problems are violent and unpredictable.
   Fact: While some people who suffer from mental health issues do commit antisocial acts, a mental health issue does not equal criminality or violence - despite the media's tendency to emphasize a suspected link. People with mental illness are no more likely to commit violence than anyone in the general public, but they are more likely to be victimized and are more likely to inflict violent actions on themselves.

Myth: Mental health issues happen because of bad parenting or personal weakness.
   Fact: The main risk factors for mental health issues are not bad parenting or personal weakness but rather genetics, severe and prolonged stress (such as physical or sexual abuse), or other environmental influences (such as birth trauma or head injury).

Myth: Treatments for mental health issues is not usually effective.
   Fact: The effectiveness of any treatment depends on a number of factors including the type of mental issue and the particular needs of the individual. A combination of psychiatric medication and psychotherapy, or social interventions are the most effective way to treat mental health issues.

Myth: Mental health issues are caused by everyday stressors.
   Fact: It may seem that stress is responsible for mental health issues; however, there is no one clear cause of mental health issues. Rather, it is a result of complex interactions between psychological, biological, genetic and social factors. Stress, stigma, and lack of support can make it worse for the individual.

Myth: Mental health issues are always hereditary.
   Fact: Some mental health issues include a genetic component, which results in a predisposition or vulnerability toward the illness among children and siblings, but environment also plays a key role in the development of certain mental health issues. If someone in one's family has mental health issucs, that person will be at higher risk.

If you start to experience the symptoms of a mental health issue, it is important for you to see a medical professional to determine if you have a problem that will require treatment. If you know of anyone who seems to have symptoms of a mental health issue, urge that person to do the same.

Managing Trauma Workbook

Coping with the Stigma of a Mental Health Issue

Get treatment. Don't let the fear of being labeled with a mental health issue prevent you from seeking help. Treatment can provide relief by identifying and reducing symptoms that interfere with your work and personal life. How can you get treatment? _____
_____
_____
_____

Don't let stigma create self-doubt and shame. If you are buying into the stigma, you will have the mistaken belief that your issue is a sign of personal weakness, or that you should be able to control it better. How can you have less self-doubt? _____
_____
_____
_____

How can you have less shame? _____
_____
_____
_____

Don't isolate yourself. Have the courage to confide in your family members, friends, partner, clergy, therapist, or other members of your community. Who can you reach out to and who can you trust for the compassion, support and understanding you need? _____
_____
_____
_____

Get help at work. If you are having unwanted stress after experiencing a trauma and it is affecting your work, confidentially talk with your supervisor, explain what you are doing to help yourself, and find out what plans and programs are available that might help. _____
_____
_____
_____

If you and others are willing, share responses.